Precision Marketing

Precision Marketing

The New Rules for Attracting, Retaining, and Leveraging Profitable Customers

Jeff Zabin and Gresh Brebach

WILEY

John Wiley & Sons, Inc.

Published by John Wiley & Sons, Inc., Hoboken, New Jersey.
Published simultaneously in Canada.

For general information on our other products and services, or technical support, please contact our Customer Care Department within the United States at (800) 762-2974, outside the United States at (317) 572-3993 or fax (317) 572-4002.

Designations used by companies to distinguish their products are often claimed by trademarks. In all instances where the author or publisher is aware of a claim, the product names appear in Initial Capital letters. Readers, however, should contact the appropriate companies for more complete information regarding trademarks and registration.

Wiley also publishes its books in a variety of electronic formats. Some content that appears in print may not be available in electronic books. For more information about Wiley products, visit our web site at www.wiley.com.

Library of Congress Cataloging-in-Publication Data:

Zabin, Jeff.
   Precision marketing : the new rules for attracting, retaining, and leveraging profitable customers / Jeff Zabin and Gresh Brebach.
      p. cm.
   Includes bibliographical references and index.
     ISBN 0-471-46761-8 (cloth)
  1. Marketing. I. Brebach, Gresh. II. Title.
   HF5415.Z33   2004
   658.8—dc22   2003020240

Printed in the United States of America.

10 9 8 7 6 5 4 3 2 1

In fond memory of my grandparents Louis and Rose Binstein,
corner grocers in Council Bluffs, Iowa. For them,
precision marketing was merely second nature.
—JSZ

To Judy, whose perseverance has lasted a lifetime.
—GTB

CONTENTS

ACKNOWLEDGMENTS

T his book came together relatively quickly. Our enthusiasm for the subject matter played an important role. In addition, we're indebted to a number of people whose assistance greatly facilitated the effort. At the top of the list is Scott Hess, researcher, writer, and futurist extraordinaire. His contributions to the last couple of chapters, in particular, helped raise the caliber of the book as a whole.

We would like to thank our hundreds of colleagues in the Global Marketing Solutions group at Fair Isaac who share our passion for the power of precision marketing. Special thanks to Tom McEnery, Richard Howe, Gordon Cameron, Jane Johnson, Chris Leitz, and Shelley Ehrman.

A large number of marketing executives challenged and educated us along our journey of discovery. While they are too many to name individually, we would like to thank a few who played an integral role in advancing our thinking. They include Dan Collins (CMO, Ritz-Carlton), Bill Duffy (Senior Director, Market Research, Kraft Foods), Bryan Finke (VP, Interactive Marketing, Nike), Vickie Jones (SVP, Marketing, SBC Communications), Rob Solomon (SVP, Marketing, Outrigger Hotels and Resorts), Bill Mirbach (VP, Direct Marketing, Intuit), Randy Quinn (SVP, Brand Development, Unilever), Mike Dobbs (VP, Product Marketing, Cingular), and Bill Bean (Director of Channel and Customer Insight, Pepsi-Cola Company).

In addition, we're grateful to Marc Landsberg (EVP, Corporate

Strategy, Publicis Groupe) and Scott Moore (SVP, Decision Sciences, Leo Burnett) for sharing their insights from a global agency perspective. Thanks also to Sunil Garga (President, Marketing Management Analytics), Tim Armstrong (VP, Marketing, Google), and Rick Mansfield (CMO, Catalina Marketing Corporation) for deepening our understanding of marketing mix modeling, content targeting, and behavior-based marketing services, respectively.

Mohan Sawhney is a constant source of inspiration, and many of our ideas were informed by our previous collaborations. Of course, we're grateful to Phil Kotler, not only for writing the Foreword to this book, but also for the immeasurable impact that his work has had on the field of marketing as a whole. Also, thanks to Russ Maney, Bill Kahn, Mark Turchan, Eric Cohen, Phyllis Zabin, and Ruben Shohet for their insights and feedback.

Many thanks to our literary agent, Helen Rees, as well as to the editorial, production, and marketing folks at Wiley. They include Airié Stuart, Emily Conway, and Linda Witzling. Finally, thanks to Jacqueline Shohet Zabin for her support and encouragement throughout the writing of this book. She deserves the biggest credit roll of all.

FOREWORD

Suppose your company is like most other companies, capable of producing many more goods than it can possibly sell. This is clearly today's plight in the auto, steel, and electronics industries—and in countless other industries, as well.

In fact, between late 2001 and late 2003, industrial production rose 5 percent, even as companies eliminated more than a million jobs. That companies today can produce far more goods with far fewer employees has led many economists to predict that the unemployment rate and per capita income in this country will remain relatively unchanged for the next several years, even if the economy should grow by a healthy 4 or 5 percent a year.

In many markets, the extraordinary gain in productivity has led to a condition of customer scarcity and hypercompetition. It's a condition that has forced major marketers to confront a new set of challenges. The biggest challenge is, simply, "How can we rescue our brand from decline other than to cut prices—to the point that it may no longer make economic sense to even stay in business?"

In the 1960s, the answer to intensified competition was to increase the amount of spending on TV commercials and other forms of advertising and promotion. And, by and large, it worked! People were drawn to the magic of television. They were mesmerized by the "man in the street" and "product as hero" selling spots, no matter how formulaic, and these commercials greatly influenced their purchase decisions. Companies that invested heavily in 60-second commercials could often count on creating brand franchises that would produce huge returns on their investments. In some cases, it was almost a foregone conclusion.

Now, of course, we live in a different world, with a different set of norms. One need only consider the systematic decline in the perceived value of most major brands. In the past, a well-known national brand could usually command a 15 to 30 percent premium over average competitor brands; today it may be lucky to fetch a 5 to 15 percent premium. This is especially true in the grocery aisle. According to ACNielsen, unit sales of store-brand goods grew 8.6 percent between 2001 and 2003, versus only 1.5 percent for national brands.

Brands are languishing. Similarly, as I suggested, what worked yesterday in terms of mass marketing doesn't work today to nearly the same effect. The reasons are myriad. For one thing, fewer people are watching TV—or at least they are not paying as much attention to the commercials. Using new technologies, many viewers are zapping the commercials altogether, and many more people will do so in the future. Moreover, with a hundred TV channels in every home and a dozen magazines in every mailbox, there's a great deal more clutter, making it harder than ever for marketers to reach their target audiences with any degree of efficiency.

Yet, paradoxically, companies are scrambling to buy TV commercials in 30- and even 15-second intervals, sometimes at several hundred thousand dollars a pop, in record numbers. Why? Because buying commercial time on broadcast television is a deeply ingrained behavior in corporate America. It's been the way of the world for more than half a century. And, as everyone knows all too well, old habits die hard.

Indeed, many corporate marketers persist in thinking that the traditional approach to mass media marketing remains perfectly sound. It's not that they're blind to the world around them. Rather, they're stuck in a fixed mind set. They have become prisoners of what they know. As a result, their marketing allocation decisions have often tended to become frozen in time. If mass media ad campaigns accounted for 90 percent of a company's marketing budget in 1985, for example, then these campaigns may well account for that same percentage today. No matter that the business outcomes are bound to be far less impressive in a world where building substantial brand awareness through traditional channels has become a hundred times harder.

Part of the problem is that many marketing organizations are skilled in only the four traditional marketing activities: *market research, advertising, sales promotion,* and *sales force.* Often, they have failed to acquire (or attain, on an outsourced basis) the capabilities that are required to succeed in today's technology-driven marketing environment. These skills and capabilities include customer relationship management (CRM), partner relationship management (PRM), database marketing and data mining, integrated marketing communications, and profitability analysis by product, segment, customer, and channel.

Meanwhile, in the face of steadily declining profits, CEOs and CFOs are finally demanding accountability from their marketing organizations. They want to see tangible results—not only in the form of increased brand awareness, but also in the form of real dollars on the plus side of the balance sheet. For the first time, the executive boardroom is being dominated by talk of "Marketing ROI." They see waste when a cat food ad reaches mostly non–cat owners and an acne medicine reaches non–acne face owners. They wonder if certain actions might be taken to minimize the waste.

Where, indeed, should companies spend money to reduce their glutted inventories? Several answers have been offered. One answer is to spend more on R&D, in an effort to introduce new lines of innovative products, rather than more of the same. Another answer is to improve the quality of existing products, especially in response to consumer feedback and a deep understanding of their unmet needs. Still another answer is to improve customer service, which these days is getting to be as important as the product itself. Another set of answers calls for shifting some money from advertising to public relations, sponsorships, and event marketing as a way to drive brand awareness—again, with a line of sight to achieving an incremental lift in sales revenues.

Finally, there is another answer. It's one that Jeff Zabin and co-author Gresh Brebach address so perceptively in this book. *Put more money into gaining a better understanding of your customers and prospects, and then market to them in a targeted way!* Put an end to the hit-or-miss approach of mass marketing. Blanketing everyone in the universe with the same broad message is simply not a smart way to do business.

After all, not all customers are the same. They differ greatly in terms of their demographics, lifestyles, needs, perceptions, preferences, and behaviors. Marketers can't afford to treat them as a homogenous group. Instead, marketers need to know the current profitability of each customer segment, and even each individual customer, as well as their potential lifetime profitability.

Marketers also need to understand customers' specific wants and needs. And they then need to market to them in a differentiated manner, based on that understanding. Admittedly, it's not an entirely new message. Leading thinkers have touched on the same theme in the context of CRM, one-to-one marketing, and database marketing for much of the past decade.

Yet *Precision Marketing* is the first book to bring such clarity and insight to the topic, and to frame it in the proper context (which is technology and data analytics). In his previous book, Jeff Zabin demonstrated his skill at applying universal wisdom to contemporary business. In this book, he and Brebach do the same thing. For example, they transcend the argument of one-to-one versus mass marketing, as well as creative/intuitive marketing versus scientific/database marketing, by realizing that the truth isn't in the black or the white. Rather, the truth is always in the gray, and these seemingly opposing marketing forces can be reconciled to a company's competitive advantage.

Today, the promise of precision marketing—*delivering the right message at the right time through the right channel to the right people*—is more than possible, thanks to recent advances in technology and the infusion of a scientific approach. In fact, marketing *must* integrate a strong precision marketing component—combining rifle marketing with shotgun marketing—and, in the process, become more accountable for its impact on shareholder value. Done right, precision marketing can improve a company's productivity and profitability by orders of magnitude.

I would recommend this book as the best first stopping place for anyone in management wanting to gain insights into the emerging trends of what I call "new marketing." You will learn how marketing is evolving. In particular, you will learn how precision marketing is being used effectively by such companies as Kraft Foods, Unilever, Tesco (the leading U.K. supermarket chain), the Royal Bank of Canada, and SBC Communications, among others. No doubt the collective insights will help shape the future of your own marketing program.

Writing in a lively fashion with good theory and stories, Zabin and Brebach address many of the key questions faced by companies today. For example:

~ How can my company capture useful data on individual customers?

~ How can my company integrate the data from different databases to get a 360-degree view of our customers?

~ How can my company mine the data to derive rich insights into customer segments and trends as well as individual customers?

~ How can my company measure the sales and profit resulting from having invested in precision marketing?

My test of a good book is whether I learned anything new and useful, above and beyond a bunch of catchy terms—which, in the case of *Precision Marketing*, includes such gems as *promiscuous consumption, blueprinting the ideal customer, SiloSync, the director of marketing economics*, and *the consensual customer*. If my five pages of notes are any indication, this book passes the test with flying colors.

—Philip Kotler
S.C. Johnson Distinguished Professor
of International Marketing
Kellogg School of Management
Northwestern University

INTRODUCTION

"Our employees are instructed to treat every customer . . . exactly as they would like to be treated were they in the customer's place and the customer in ours," reads the 1900 edition of Sears, Roebuck and Company's *Consumers Guide*, the forerunner of the catalog that would become a fixture in American homes through most of the past century. "If you favor us with your patronage," it continues, "we will do everything in our power to merit your trade."

Sound familiar? In a world transformed by the growth of enterprises and the rise of modern transportation, and by technologies that have reduced transaction costs and created new communication channels that allow people to interact in ways that could hardly be imagined in 1900, such proclamations have recently resurfaced as a universal fight song.

Today, of course, it's no mean feat to "merit the trade" of new customers, let alone retain the ones that already exist. Just ask Sears, which has been severely battered in recent years by customer attrition, declining sales, and lower profits. In an effort to reverse its lackluster performance, the nation's number three retailer is spending almost $1 billion a year on advertising, using mass media vehicles to communicate a mostly undifferentiated marketing message (its latest tagline: *Sears. Good life. Great price.*) to a target audience that consists of just about everyone. All we can say is, "Good luck."

Clearly, Sears is stuck in a rut where no company today can

afford to be: spending a lot of money on mass media marketing in a desperate attempt to create measurable results. Unfortunately, without a discernible niche, mass media marketing may be Sears' only option.

Not so for companies with more narrowly defined marketing messages and target audiences. For these companies, a new set of tools and capabilities—which, taken together, enable a business process called *precision marketing*—promises to increase marketing effectiveness, drive shareholder value, and fundamentally change the way senior executives run their marketing organizations. And not a moment too soon.

THE WAY WE LIVE (AND SHOP) NOW

In this Introduction, we look at the changing consumer landscape to help explain the growing infatuation that today's corporate leaders are having with *precision marketing*—a term which, for now, can be simply described as a technology-enabled process for capturing and managing customer data, analyzing that data to derive strategic insights, and using those insights to drive more efficient and profitable customer interactions. The context begins with a simple compelling fact: We live in an unprecedented era of customer scarcity. Information technology—combined with new business processes for how companies buy, make, and sell—has played a major role in creating this reality.

Technology, in particular, has produced such amazing efficiencies in the use of labor and materials that supply now outstrips demand across a wide array of markets. In virtually every category, it seems, an overabundance of merchandise is going nowhere fast, parked on shipping docks, gathering dust in warehouses, and standing idle on showroom floors. Simply put: *There ain't enough good customers to go around.*

As a consequence, companies are left with a pie that has essentially reached its maximum circumference where customer growth is concerned. This is true even in technology markets, where manufacturers have traditionally enjoyed rapid turnover. A case in point is the personal computer industry. In 2002, the *New York Times* reported that, more than any time in its 27-year history, the industry has found itself in a quandary, having to concoct new reasons to persuade the world's 500 million PC owners to replace their existing machines. In short, the first years of the new century have given birth to a business climate in which replacement cycles have faltered, manufacturing plants have overproduced, and warehouses (or *pipes*, in the case of telecom providers) have become saddled with excess capacity.

To make matters worse, brand loyalty has become ever more fleeting. And driving brand loyalty has become ever more expensive. One wonders: How can a company hope to build brand loyalty in an environment where consumers are continuously confronted by an enormous number of choices? Consider the beverage category, which introduced approximately 11,000 new SKUs in 2002 alone. "The algebra will tell you that your shares are going to get diluted in an environment like that," notes Bill Bean, director of Channel and Customer Insight at Pepsi-Cola Company—which, for its part, introduced approximately 100 new SKUs in 2002.[1]

Many consumers today readily switch allegiance to any brand that offers what they judge to be the best value for their money, regardless of their—or their parents'—past buying behavior. "Once a customer, always a customer" was a nice motto in its time. But it has little connection to today's world, where the experience of having grown up with a certain brand seldom translates into a long-term sentimental, let alone economic, attachment. Favorable reviews from a friend about a competing product or service, the arrival of an enticing promotional offer, or even a spontaneous thirst for adventure might provide a sufficiently valid excuse to break off a decades-old relationship.

One might rightfully conclude that we've entered a world of *promiscuous consumption*. "Today I'll buy this brand," shrugs Joe

Consumer, "and tomorrow I'll buy a different brand." But while such a world may suit Joe Consumer just fine, given his open desire to play the field, it can be an inhospitable place for companies that would much prefer long-term fidelity over the business equivalent of a one-night stand.

Notwithstanding the staggering number of books and articles written on the topic in recent years, brand loyalty is easily understood. It arises from a customer's belief in the relative superiority of a product or service, as reaffirmed by its repeated use over time, thereby fulfilling expectations around consistency. In this way, one might argue that brand loyalty often goes hand in hand with complacency. In some cases, it endures due to the simple fact that human beings tend to abhor change and embrace familiarity.

Brand loyalty used to be easily won. Some families were Ford families. Some families were Crest, Skippy, and Tide families. A brand was almost like a political affiliation. As long as it performed reasonably well and was advertised heavily enough, people would continue to buy it. Usually, a leading brand could do no wrong. These days, on the other hand, people are constantly testing the limits of their brand loyalty with a simple question: *What have you done for me lately?* With increasing frequency, they're coming to an equally simple conclusion: *Not enough.*

Why do today's brands need to work so hard to win us over? Is it because, as a society, we've become more demanding? Less committed? More open to change? Whatever the reason, we're bearing witness to the systematic decline of brand loyalty. For compelling evidence, look no further than Kraft Foods, the largest food and beverage company in North America, with products that regularly find their way into 99 percent of all households. Kraft defines a loyal customer as a person who bought more than 70 percent of the same brand within a category over the past three years. Three decades ago, the percentage of Kraft's customers believed to fit this description was approximately 40 percent, on average. Today it's said to hover somewhere around 15 percent.

Paradoxically, Kraft appears to be doing just fine, thank you, owing to its extensive roster of so-called "category killers." To name just a few: Kraft macaroni & cheese, which holds an 82 percent share of the market, Philadelphia cream cheese, with a 67 percent share, and Ritz crackers, with a 51 percent share. So what's the problem? No problem, other than the fact that Kraft pays dearly to maintain its dominant market position, spending roughly $850 million a year on advertising and other forms of marketing promotion. For a company the size of Kraft, it's an awful lot of money.

The reason Kraft allocates the lion's share of its resources to advertising and other forms of marketing promotion—about 42 cents of every dollar it earns—is easy to understand. Kraft needs to reach as many shoppers as possible, on an ongoing basis, and convince them that its brands are worth the extra dime, quarter, or dollar relative to neighboring brands that occupy the same shelf space. But shouldn't customers already be convinced? After all, most of Kraft's category killers have been on the market for years, some for decades. Why would smart shoppers need continual reminding of their own brand preferences—unless, like that odd little fish in the 2003 movie *Finding Nemo*, they suffer en masse from momentary bouts of amnesia? Of course, we've already revealed the answer: Kraft's loyal fan base is dwindling. Promotion-sensitive consumers now account for the bulk of its sales revenues. As if it were any consolation, Kraft is hardly alone. Many companies can only bemoan the fact that their former ranks of never-settle-for-less customers now teeter on the verge of extinction.

BEHOLD THE GENERIC REVOLUTION

At least part of the reason for the erosion of brand loyalty relates to the proliferation of comparable market alternatives for practically everything under the sun. Call it *the attack of the clones*, in homage to another movie—the 2002 *Star Wars* prequel.

The laminated sign people are used to seeing behind the pharmacy pickup counter says it all: "You can trust generic equivalents, which offer the same high quality at a lower price." The sign now applies to practically every category of merchandise in the store. Lesser-known brands with unfamiliar labels and nonexistent advertising budgets—which, as it turns out, are not necessarily inferior to their brand-name counterparts—are gaining the attention they arguably deserve.

A particularly alarming development facing brand managers is the rapid growth of private-label store brands with names like Our Compliments, Kirkland, Safeway Select, Sam's Choice, and President's Choice. In fact, the store-name brands have already become a formidable market force, their unit sales having more than quadrupled between 2001 and 2003. Wal-Mart's Ol Roy dog chow now outsells Purina. Nearly half the merchandise sold at Target carries the name of a store brand. Rite Aid added 250 private-label products in 2003. The trend is even reflected in the recent decision by Barnes & Noble to launch its own brand of low-cost books, expected to account for 12 percent of total revenues by 2008. In 2003, *Fortune* magazine reported that one in five items sold in U.S. stores is now store branded, while in Europe that figure has reached *two* in five items.[2] For retailers, it means 10 percent higher profits, on average. For many marketers, however, it means paring the number of brands in their portfolios and concentrating their spending on the few that already command the highest market share.

By now, practically every national brand has been supplemented by a copycat version that looks, smells, tastes, and/or feels almost identical, or that has nearly the same core characteristics. It's a reality, even if some brands may refuse to accept it. Take Oreos, for example. "You can make a cookie without trans fat but what you're trading off is the unique taste and texture that people have come to expect," explained a Kraft spokesperson, in defending the use of hydrogenated oils to make the number one selling cookie in the world. Yet anyone participating in a blind taste test would surely attest to the fact that the "unique taste and texture" of Oreos is anything but unique. The same taste and texture masquerade quite convincingly in several Oreo knockoffs. What can't you find in these rival brands? Simple. The word "Oreo."

Yet to many people, for whatever reason, a package of Oreos is worth an extra buck. Some people would never consider buying faux Oreos when they could buy the real McCoy. But, to quote comedian Jerry Seinfeld: "Who are these people?"

More importantly, how can a company like Kraft focus its considerable marketing resources on reaching others just like them? For its part, Kraft has traditionally spent a lot of money in its efforts to coax *all* current and potential cookie aficionados in the right direction, all the while knowing full well that many recipients of its marketing messages are going to be poor prospects. A lot of them may not even buy cookies in the first place.

Granted, some entrenched superbrands are destined to retain their positions as category leaders, if only by virtue of their names. The brand equity enshrined in the name Coca-Cola will likely live on forever, and always be worth a gazillion dollars to the investor community. Brand equity helps explain how Coke, for more than a century the most recognized trademark in the world, can maintain a ubiquitous presence when only about 16 cents of every dollar it earns is spent on advertising and promotions. (Interestingly, most of the company's recent growth has come from strong sales of its noncarbonated drinks, including bottled water.)

The so-called "aspirational quality" of brands explains why many people will continue to pay a hefty premium for cups of Starbucks coffee and scoops of Ben & Jerry's ice cream (growing up, they could never afford such luxuries). Aspiration—combined with the "trust factor"—explains why many people will always insist on buying Bayer aspirin, and paying more for it than for generic aspirin, despite knowing full well that the two are exactly the same. And because money is no object when it comes to prestige, people will continue to buy Tiffany jewelry and Godiva chocolate, and pay top dollar for the latest in brands of designer clothes and accessories, fueling the trillion-dollar fashion industry.

Consumers will never become completely brand blind. Or, to put it another way, brand is not dead, only resting. Right? One thing is certain: The fear of brand death continues to hang over the advertising industry like a dark cloud, and for good reason. Marketers can point to April 2, 1993, as a milestone in the history of the generic revolution. On that date, Philip Morris cut the price of its Marlboro cigarettes, a premium brand marketed to the American public for nearly four decades, to compete with a handful of no-name bargain brands that had begun to capture significant market share. Also on that date, Wall Street gave in to an overactive imagination. It responded to the Marlboro announcement by driving down not only Philip Morris' stock price but also that of many other leading consumer goods companies, including Quaker Oats, Heinz, and Procter & Gamble, whose core assets mainly consisted of the brand equity embedded in their household name products. Market doomsayers declared that the downfall of "the brand"—whose value, they asserted, had been kept artificially inflated through a never-ending series of elaborate image-building schemes, carried out by expensive advertising campaigns—was firmly upon us, and that the marketplace for consumer goods would never be the same.

They were wrong, of course, but only to a degree. Yes, the stock prices recovered and the doomsayers retreated. But the lesson of that day—that brand loyalty can be highly precarious and should be handled with care—lingers on a decade later. On July 11, 2003, Moody's Investors Service released a major report warning that the generic brands of deep-discount cigarette makers were wiping out the ability of the major players to raise prices and preserve profit margins. Among those taking the biggest hit in terms of erosion in operating performance and credit ratings: Philip Morris and its Marlboro brand.

The trend is clear. As the availability of buyer options increases, the degree of market differentiation declines, and the level of product superiority becomes less clear, brand loyalty will continue to go out the window on many fronts. Capricious consumer behavior will, in turn, leave companies with little choice but to incur the added expense of doing a lot more coaxing. This means more TV commercials. More radio spots. More magazine ads. More in-store displays. More event sponsorships. More highway billboards. More mass mailings. More wasted money.

Alternatively, companies can harness the power of highly refined consumer targeting to accelerate the growth and profitability of their brands, as many are now beginning to do, with escalating levels of organizational vigor and resource commitment. They can embark on technology-enabled brand-building programs that adopt more efficient and effective ways to market to the *right* consumers—that is, those people who are already predisposed to buying the product or service at hand, and who help drive corporate profitability—while mitigating the cost of marketing to the *wrong* consumers. The wrong consumers are people who would never, under any ordinary set of circumstances, make a purchase decision, no matter how many times the best of all possible marketing messages was waved in their faces. In essence, this is the difference between working hard and working smart, and it serves as the main focus of this book.

TAKING UP ARMS AGAINST A SEA OF TROUBLES

The proliferation of market alternatives is one phenomenon that has sent brand companies running for cover. Beyond that, other forces are also converging to fundamentally change the dynamics of consumer shopping behavior.

One such force is the advent of Internet search functionality for comparison shopping. Price transparency leads to increased price competition as suppliers invariably find themselves being pitted against one another along price variables. The insurance industry offers a good example of this phenomenon at work, and the havoc that it can wreak on the top lines of countless businesses. Using data on individual life insurance policies, researchers found that a 10 percent increase in the share of individuals using the Internet for price comparison reduces average insurance prices by as much as five percent.[3]

Another potent force remaking the consumer landscape is the large-scale migration of shopping traffic away from upscale department stores—those that charge a premium for such frivolities as pleasant ambiance and pretty displays—and toward no-frills discount chains such as Wal-Mart, Target, and Costco. Known for keeping overhead so low that margins never exceed 14 percent, Costco saw its sales double between 1998 and 2003, to almost $40 billion. Meanwhile, Federated Department Stores, along with many other high-end retailers, reported substantial earning declines during the same period. A weakening economy was only partly to blame. As more people adopt a sensibility that emphasizes cost savings, the upscale department stores will become increasingly less crowded—unless, that is, they can find a way to invigorate their business and recapture their former glory. To that end, U.S. department stores are today spending more than a billion dollars on renovations (Federated alone budgeted $300 million to refurbish its aging Macy's stores), hoping to create a "shopping experience" that outweighs the cost savings offered by the discount chains.

Will expensive renovations save the department store from extinction or simply create retail museums? The important point is that, with new customers hard to find and existing ones fickle and easily spooked, many companies today are resolving to do everything in their power to—again, in the words of that 1900 edition of the Sears *Consumers Guide*—"merit the trade" of their customers.

Of course, the most sure way to move more merchandise off the floor is to do what sales managers have done since the invention of the black marker: Hack away at the price tag. Price reductions tend to make the cash register ring—especially today, with consumers on the whole more price sensitive than ever. Market researchers can perform conjoint analysis exercises until they're blue in the face. Marketing departments can come up with new ways to bundle value-added services and to quantify the economic benefits of nonprice variables. But in the end, all things being equal, cost is going to be the key determinant for a large number of purchase decisions.

The intensification of price competition naturally leads to a downward spiral of ever-increasing markdowns. Yet here's where companies need to exercise caution, lest they fall into the Big Mac-versus-Whopper trap of profit erosion, from whence there's no return. So, while standard marketing strategy may dictate that companies do everything possible to maintain market share, the validity of this approach is open to question in today's world, given the high cost of going down the low-cost road. Sales for the sake of sales can be a lethal prescription if the profit component is altogether missing. As one media consultant recently put it: "Over the past five years we've seen mature core brands suffocate under their own weight like lost, beached whales on the shores of EDLP (every day low price) Beach."[4]

Price competition tends to spur marketing creativity. And today companies can offer their customers more creative ways than ever to save money—and even possibly to *win* money (or other valuable prizes), given the endless array of new possibilities around promotions. Often elaborate in their design and execution, online sweepstakes, in particular, have become a popular marketing vehicle. "Register at Huggies.com to win a year's supply of diapers and baby wipes." "Register at Kohls.com to win a $1,000 shopping spree." "Register at SpikeTV.com to win the Ultimate Guy Vacation."

Which isn't to say that good old print coupons have fallen by the wayside. On the contrary: Once seen as a pastime dominated by working-class families who would take scissors to the Sunday circulars as a way to put additional morsels of food on the table, coupon clipping in America today has evolved into an almost fashionable enterprise. *The coupon culture* now pervades practically all ranks of society. Even well-heeled shoppers boast of the "instant savings" they enjoyed by redeeming their "private sale invitations." In 1965, one-half of Americans were coupon users. Today, the percentage approaches 90 percent. Retailers used more coupons, rebates, and sweepstakes to attract customers to their doors during the holiday shopping season of 2002 than during any previous holiday shopping season. The enthusiasm for coupons, rebates, and sweepstakes—as well as loyalty points—represents an enormous opportunity for companies in the context of precision marketing, as we see in Chapter 2, given the need to capture individual customer profile information.

For big-ticket items, discount offers are usually served up in the form of "major incentive packages." A striking example of historic high spending on such packages was touted by the Big Three automakers beginning in late 2001, when zero interest financing boosted their combined fourth quarter sales by more than half a million units. Starting with General Motors, the automakers had planned to offer these loans for a limited time, and then only on a few less-popular models, as a surefire way to clear dealer lots of rapidly depreciating inventory. Instead, the automakers found themselves extending and broadening the offers—at times even sweetening the pot with generous cash rebates and six-month payment deferrals—over the next two years as the expected recovery of the economy failed to materialize and customer demand continued to sputter. By August 2003, incentive packages averaged $2,630, and zero interest financing appeared to have become a permanent feature of the marketing landscape.

Not just automakers; major appliance dealers, furniture makers, and a host of other companies facing similarly weak demand, and otherwise unable to free themselves from the clutches of a recession that continued to drag on, followed suit, posting NO MONEY DOWN and BUY NOW, PAY LATER placards in their own windows. Before long, the parade of too-good-to-be-true offers seemed to stretch as far as the eye could see. Payment flexibility became the norm for the purchase of virtually any type of product or service, from apparel and furnishings to home remodeling and vacation packages. (Want to spend a week in the Greek Islands while minimizing the pain of having to fork out all that dough? No problem. Book your package through Sears Travel. You won't be charged until the billing date of the month in which you depart. Plus, you can pay in 12 equal payments spread out over the course of the year, all interest-free. What's more, you will automatically receive Sears Club Points that can be redeemed for new luggage, swimsuits, and designer sunglasses.)

Good for the consumer but bad for the merchant. Any storyline that culminates in a decision to offer zero interest financing might be said to resemble a drama of almost Shakespearean proportions. As the Prince of Denmark himself might have observed, companies have only two choices: "to suffer the slings and arrows of outrageous fortune"—in other words, do nothing, which could damage shareholder value—or "to take up arms against a sea of troubles, and by opposing end them." For automakers, taking up arms meant paying interest rates of nearly 5 percent to finance those hundreds of thousands of no-interest loans. By some estimates, this incentive alone translated into an astounding $2,600 hit to the bottom line for every

$20,000 vehicle sold. It's no surprise, then, that the Chrysler Group of DaimlerChrysler reportedly made only $226 per vehicle sold in 2002, while the Ford Motor Company actually *lost* an average of $114 on every vehicle sold that year.

Needless to say, such generosity can be too expensive to sustain indefinitely. Sooner or later, as we have already suggested, companies need to step off the slippery slope of price concessions. This means, in addition to improving the "shopping experience," focusing on customer service and satisfaction as competitive points of differentiation. Let's face it: Companies can afford to pay less attention to customer satisfaction when new customers are lining up at the door, wallets wide open. Yet just the opposite holds true when markets are saturated and growth has slowed to a pitiful crawl.

A luxury hotel chain like the Ritz-Carlton naturally places a premium on providing high touch, state-of-the-art customer care. "We engender customer loyalty by delivering on personalized customer experience," notes Dan Collins, the chief marketing officer.[5] It's in the company's DNA. However, the concept may be somewhat less familiar to companies slugging it out in increasingly commoditized markets where alternatives abound and the lowest price generally wins the day. Yet the quality of customer service can ultimately become the decisive factor in who gets the gold.

Consider the mobile phone market. How can a service provider create a basis for differentiation when every competitor offers essentially the same choice of service plans with essentially the same set of features at essentially the same price points utilizing essentially the same types of equipment, network infrastructure, and functionality? More downloadable games, ring tones, and screensavers? More celebrity endorsements? Another namesake sports arena? Again, upping the ante on customer service—along with constant innovation—may be the best overall solution for the problem of commoditization and falling prices. The insight is nicely captured in the new tagline for U.S. Cellular: *Award-winning customer service. It's a feature, never an option.*

With customer acquisition hard to achieve and customer defection their worst enemy, companies have to meet or exceed customer expectations on an ongoing basis—again, not only through improved product quality but also through improved service quality. At a minimum, this means making Customer Appreciation Month a yearlong celebration. It also means creating better solutions through partner integration. In the move toward increased partnering—including business process outsourcing, which allows core business functions to be managed by third parties—companies are becoming part of a broader solution that involves a greater number of handoffs. Yet despite this reality, many companies continue to maintain a door-to-door approach: "My door to your door, and after that you're on your own." It's a counterproductive approach in the context of precision marketing, as we explain in Chapter 4.

WHY THIS BOOK—AND WHAT'S INSIDE

In 1900, when that edition of the Sears *Consumers Guide* was published, the average U.S. resident could go weeks without seeing an advertisement. Marketers spent the modern-day equivalent of $450 million that year on advertising and other forms of marketing promotion—again, less than half the current advertising budget for Sears alone. Today, the average person can hardly help but encounter thousands of advertisements on a daily basis. In 2002, marketers spent approximately $234 billion on advertising and other forms of marketing promotion—for the most part, using the modern-day equivalents of those same mass media vehicles.

Was the money well spent? As we've already suggested, the answer is *no*, not by a long shot. In fact, massive waste and inefficiencies have become the acceptable byproducts of modern-day marketing tactics. In a recent survey, hundreds of agency and brand executives went so far as to state that the marketing planning process is fundamentally broken and in need of a total overhaul.[6] Of course it doesn't help that, as of this writing, the economy appears only now to be slowly emerging from a three-year hangover following the 1990s boom. The economic downturn took an especially heavy toll on marketing organizations. It placed marketing programs under heavy scrutiny while forcing chief marketing officers to find new ways to stretch their dollars, tie their future spending more tightly to sales potential, and capitalize on their existing technology and data assets. The pressure to demonstrate the effectiveness of marketing investments had never been greater than during the first few years of the new millennium.

At the same time, a growing number of leading marketers have come to understand that a primarily mass media approach to campaign management is based on legacy thinking. Such thinking fails to take into account a whole new set of possibilities, made possible by recent advances in network technology and the intelligent use of customer data, for improving overall marketing performance. This book explores some of the possibilities for applying the "scientific method" to the process of targeting high prospect customers with relevant marketing messages—in part, by showing what some of the leading, most innovative companies are already doing in terms of precision marketing.

Along the way, the book speaks to some of the most pressing issues that marketers face today, as well as some of the key trends that are changing the very role of marketing. Among them: the demise of point marketing and the rise of holistic marketing; the demise of spend-free marketing and the rise of ROI marketing; the demise of marketing guesswork and the rise of marketing science; the demise of brand management and the rise of customer relationship management; the demise of technology-*supported* marketing and the rise of technology-*enabled* marketing; and, finally, the demise of a mass-marketing-only model and the rise of a mass marketing *and* precision marketing hybrid model.

We should also be clear about what this book is *not*. Most of all, it's not a how-to book. We intentionally avoid diving too deeply into the nuts and bolts of technology platforms and implementation. And while we're quick to sing the praises of database-enabled analytics, we avoid making the intricacies of the statistical equations a primary focus. The reason is simple. This book is written for drivers, not mechanics. Drivers need to know how their vehicles are going to respond under various road conditions. They need to know what qualifies as good acceleration, good handling, and a good driving experience. They need to ask the right questions of the mechanics and be able to provide feedback that spurs improved performance. But at no point do they need to get their hands dirty beneath the hood—unless, like Bill Gates, they simply can't help themselves.

The ideas in this book are organized into six chapters, as follows:

In Chapter 1, we chronicle the rise of precision marketing as an idea whose time has come. We trace the evolution of market segmentation, and put forth a concept called *blueprinting the ideal customer* to describe the next generation of market segmentation. We explore the limitations of mass marketing. At the same time, we show that precision marketing and mass marketing are complementary and should work in concert to deliver maximum value. We talk about "predictable imbalance" in terms of brand consumption, and show how precision marketing can help marketers adjust for the fact that relatively few of their customers account for a disproportionate amount of their brand's value. Finally, we discuss the power of context-sensitive marketing.

In Chapter 2, we explore the pressures companies now face in terms of resource constraints and marketing accountability, and look at the business processes that foster the growth of profitable customer relationships. We approach these processes by harking back to the classic Plan-Do-Act-Check cycle, with its roots in Renaissance thinking. Applied to marketing, the cycle becomes a closed loop design in which strategy, technology, and implementation all come together, the basic premise being that companies need to treat every customer interaction as part of a continuous learning process. We discuss how some leading companies are already applying the principles of the precision marketing cycle, particularly in the context of offline-to-online marketing campaigns.

In Chapter 3, we explain that customer data integration is a precondition to predictive analytics, which in turn is a precondition to precision marketing. We show how analytics can be used to predict future customer preferences, match offerings to customer wants and needs, and create the messages that are most likely to elicit a favorable response. We describe how analytics can lay the foundation for a long-term relationship with customers with high future profit potential. We also outline a vision for an applications suite that encompasses all of the technologies that enable companies to better understand their customers, more effectively go to market with their offerings, and build more profitable relationships.

"To be original," wrote Paul Arden, long a creative force in the advertising industry, "seek your inspiration from unexpected sources." In Chapter 4, we do precisely that, by adopting the Gaia hypothesis as a guiding metaphor to explore the interconnections between the different components that make up an extended business network. With the rise of business process outsourcing, these interconnections can have everything to do with fostering the growth and maintenance of profitable customer relationships. In fact, for many companies, precision marketing means having access to a host of resources and capabilities that may not currently reside within the four walls of the company, but that may be readily available through partner integration.

In Chapter 5, we take a strong stance on personal privacy issues, which have recently been the subject of intense debate. Because precision marketing relies on collecting, storing, manipulating, analyzing, and acting on customer data, we argue that a smart, progressive approach to privacy is essential. In fact, the very foundation for precision marketing is an effective privacy policy that reassures customers that their data will not be misused. This was not an issue for Richard Sears when he was selling pocket watches to railroad trainmen, but it is today as privacy-sensitive marketers struggle to balance factors that include legislation, litigation, technology, and consumer choice. In our view, forward-thinking marketers will embrace a strategy that focuses on securing "consensual customers" who engage in a first-person, ongoing exchange of data in exchange for value.

Finally, in Chapter 6, we gaze into the crystal ball to behold a future that marries the intimacy of the corner shopkeeper with the scale and scope of a multidivisional enterprise, while infusing into the marriage a powerful blend of real-time analytics capabilities. We look at the future of customer loyalty programs, present a vision for a universal profile management system, and paint several futuristic scenarios. We show how, through the art and science of precision marketing, companies will create customized promotions that readily adapt to customer behavior. Finally, we explain why the year 2054, as depicted in the movie *Minority Report*, may actually be right around the corner—but in a far more palatable form.

1
THE RISE OF
PRECISION MARKETING

Be precise. A lack of precision is dangerous when the margin of error is small.

—Donald Rumsfeld

More than a thousand bombs and missiles were dropped on Baghdad, three times the number from the entire Gulf War," reported Pentagon correspondent Jim Miklaszewski, while being interviewed on *Today*. The date was March 22, 2003, two days after President George W. Bush, vowing to "disarm Iraq and to free its people," had given the order for the first strikes on the capital city after being told by the CIA it believed that it had determined the whereabouts of Saddam Hussein and other key members of his regime. Miklaszewski continued: "And this time, they're all precision-guided, deadly accurate, designed to kill only the targets, not innocent civilians."

"Precision" is a word that Americans, and most everyone else around the world, heard incessantly in the context of military operations during the initial phase of the conflict. News coverage in March and early April brought a continuous stream of commentary about the U.S.-led coalition forces' "precision bombing" campaign. Officials themselves boasted about the "pinpoint accuracy" of the 2,000-pound bombs being dropped from F-117 Nighthawk stealth fighter bombers, as well as the Tomahawk cruise missiles being fired from six U.S. Navy vessels stationed in the Mediterranean, the Red Sea, and the Persian Gulf. In the final analysis, "precision" might be said to be the defining word of this war—and of any war, for that matter, in which bombs and missiles are programmed with the exact coordinates of their targets and guided there by GPS satellites.[1]

Precision is the quality of being accurate and exact. Precision tools are used for accurate and exact measurements. Precision components adhere to a set of accurate and exact standards. Precision clocks keep accurate and exact time. This is particularly true in the case of atomic clocks, which operate on an electrical oscillator regulated by the natural vibration frequencies of cesium atoms. GPS satellites carry atomic clocks designed to gain or lose no more than one second every 32,000 years!

With *precision marketing*, the principle is much the same. By utilizing the right set of technology platforms and data analytics capabilities, and by taking a specialized approach to marketing campaign design and execution, companies—no matter how large in size or how far removed they are from the end-customer—can tap into a new source of power.

The power is the ability to deliver accurate and exact marketing messages to people at a narrow customer segment level. New parents who favor the great outdoors. Home equity borrowers eager to upgrade their major appliances. Senior golfers planning a tropical vacation. Generation Y sports enthusiasts who prefer sci-fi action flicks to romantic comedies. Female, college-educated potato chip lovers. You name it. It's a power that most marketers today possess only marginally at best, yet one that promises to be a key driver of competitive advantage in the years to come.

In some respects, precision marketing is to marketing what mass customization is to manufacturing. While mass customization gives companies the ability to offer people specially configured products, precision marketing gives companies the ability to attract people with specially configured marketing messages. Importantly, mass customization is not the same as *customization*, which means "producing a product from scratch to a customized specification." By the same token, precision marketing is not the same as *one-to-one marketing*, which means customizing a marketing message at an individual customer level. One-to-one marketing sounds like a great idea, in theory. In practice, however, it can be prohibitively expensive, unnecessary, and at times even counterproductive, as we discuss later. That said, the guiding force behind precision marketing is indeed an unfettered move toward personalization, which itself hardly ranks as a new concept.

Consider that in 1900 the corner shopkeeper in smalltown America knew all of his customers by name and had a window into their daily lives. He knew what items of merchandise they bought. He knew how much money they spent—and how much money they might eventually spend. He knew their likes and dislikes, their personal histories, and their networks of friends and family. In some cases, he may even have known their dreams for the future. The breadth and depth of the information the corner shopkeeper collected on his regular customers, simply as a function of their daily interactions, went far beyond what most companies are able to capture today.

After all, does Amazon, which calls itself "Earth's most customer-centric company"—a title it arguably deserves—really know anything about you beyond your clickstream and stated product preferences? Does Allstate, which urges customers to "plan today for a better tomorrow," have even a vague idea about your dreams for the future? Does Nordstrom, long praised for its "high touch" approach to customer care (where else can you buy a pair of shoes with mismatched sizes?), have any inkling of, say, your spouse's taste in fashion? For that matter, do most large companies even pass the test of knowing how much money you spend with them, across all of their different product lines and business units, let alone how much money you might eventually spend? In all cases, the likely answer is *no*.

Compare this to the corner shopkeeper. Owing to the extent to which he was privy to both the articulated and unarticulated wants, needs, preferences, interests, attitudes, situations, and interrelationships of those who frequented his store, the corner shopkeeper had amassed some degree of true *customer insight*. And what did he do with this vast and forever-changing store of proprietary knowledge? He entered it into a relational database—namely, his own memory—where he could access it on a just-in-time basis. In this way, he could make context-sensitive recommendations whenever the opportunity presented itself.

Today we refer to this same activity as *cross-selling* and *up-selling*. The context-sensitive aspect of it, however, is often nowhere to be found. A notable exception may indeed be Amazon—which, after all, helped pioneer the use of so-called "recommendation engines" that serve up relevant product suggestions based on various data inputs, including browsing patterns, purchase behavior, stated preferences, and the behavior of other, like-minded customers. The functionality has become an integral component of the e-commerce architectures used by many online merchants, from NetFlix, the DVD rental service, to catalog companies like J. Crew and Lands' End.

In the past, the performance of most recommendation engines received only mixed reviews. But today, the accuracy of the connections between customers and their likely purchases is steadily improving, thanks to the behind-the-scenes work of complex algorithms, as well as real human beings who cross-reference products and services in ways that automated programs have sometimes failed to understand.

Knowing what and when to sell—and, just as importantly, knowing what and when *not* to sell—are key facets of precision marketing. Mastering the knowing part is a challenge that practically every company today faces, particularly those utilizing multiple customer touchpoints and operating through multiple reseller channels. Without context-sensitivity as a cornerstone of their marketing efforts, companies run the risk of annoying their customers, and possibly even infuriating them, with unwanted and often intrusive phone calls and e-mail messages, not to mention the junk mail that piles up in the foyer. Here the danger is great. Failing to obtain additional business from existing customers is one thing. Leaving a bad taste in their mouths is quite another. It can be exceedingly hard to get rid of a bad taste.

The problem, aside from the fact that most people have a strong aversion to being the target of unsolicited sales offers (even from companies with which they already do business), is that companies often take a depersonalized, desensitized, and decontextualized approach to making these offers. They often treat all customers—old ones and new ones, strong prospects and weak prospects, heavy users and light users (let alone profitable users and unprofitable users)—in more or less the same way. Moreover, they often view customers not as people whose allegiance needs to be won over on an ongoing basis (again, by gaining a sufficiently deep understanding of their wants and needs), but as people whose money needs to be gotten hold of. This pervasive mentality is even reflected in the corporate vocabulary—"share of wallet," for example, to describe the percentage of a customer's business a company might acquire over that customer's lifetime of patronage. It's reminiscent of the old sales pep talk, where the sales manager psyches up his charges by telling them, "They've got our money. Now go and get it back from them."

The corner shopkeeper, on the other hand, didn't dare run the risk of infuriating his customers. What's more, he didn't treat all customers alike. He intuitively knew the differences between good and bad customers, and he treated each accordingly. While he was certainly in business to make money, he didn't think in terms of share of wallet. Instead, he thought in terms of *relationships*. It's a fundamentally different mind set, one that companies today would do well to embrace wholeheartedly. In many cases, their future success depends upon it.

WHAT'S A RELATIONSHIP, ANYWAY?

Pose the question to an octogenarian with a sharp memory and a keen sense of humor, and you might get a recitation of one-liners once the bread and butter of vaudeville comedians. "The secret of a happy marriage remains a secret." Or: "My wife and I were happy for twenty years; then we met." Or: "I was married by a judge; I should have asked for a jury!"[2] Or enter the word "relationship" into a search engine and see what comes up. Millions of returned links, not all of them G-rated. Romance advice. Dating advice. Marriage advice. Parenting advice. Divorce advice. Plus the chat rooms and message boards and matchmaking services, all staking out their ground in the relationship-building business arena.

This book is about relationships with customers—and, to a

lesser extent, with suppliers and partners, as well. Here we speak of relationships not in terms of holy matrimony but of corporate moneymaking. Therefore, the motivating factors are more likely to be fear and greed than the heartfelt words exchanged during a couple's wedding vows. That said, certain words, like "trust," "reliability," and "commitment," are equally relevant in both worlds.

We define a *customer relationship* as a series of repeated interactions that, if managed correctly, accumulate over time into a positive memory of experiences with a product or service—or, better yet, with a company as a whole. The art of managing relationships is the art of managing every form of interaction so as to record that positive memory. Practically every company sets out to build strong, long-term relationships with its customers. The reason that so few of them succeed today can be largely attributed to such factors as hypercompetition, overcapacity, and brand disloyalty, as we note in the Introduction. Also, customer expectations have soared to new heights. In short, *customer demand* is low, yet *customers' demands* are higher than ever. It's as if the scale and speed of the Internet have made every consumer a little less patient. "What I want, when I want it" is the rallying cry of this massively networked age.

In this respect, customers have come to resemble the children's book character Eloise, calling Room Service every five minutes with her charge-it-please insouciance. Everyone fancies themselves a prima don or donna. Everyone is a customer from hell. Everyone expects that companies will bow at their feet, cater to their every whim, and deliver benefits in ways that are faster, cheaper, more flexible, and more convenient than ever before. And what happens when companies fall short of such expectations? That's when good customers, always comparison-shopping, forever deluged by competitive offers, become ex-customers.

Most companies can't afford to let that happen. Hence the Sheraton Service Promise, which can serve as a model for every company to follow. "Something not perfect?" asks a cheerful desk attendant in a recent ad campaign for the $4.5 billion hotel chain. "Just say so." The company guarantees remuneration in the form of "an instant discount, points for our rewards program, even money back" to anyone who isn't "entirely satisfied." In this context, the old adage "Keep the customer satisfied" takes on a new layer of meaning. A universal prescription for retail success, it also becomes a looming penalty for any company that fails to make the grade.

Precision marketing is about turning noncustomers into customers and turning existing customers into better customers. Think of it as the "profit center" component of a customer relationship management solution. Customer relationship management, in turn, is a combination of business processes and technologies that seek to understand customers from a multifaceted perspective, and to apply that understanding to build deeper and more profitable relationships. And how different is this modern-day objective from that of yesteryear? What's different is not the objective itself, but, rather, the challenge of realizing it—which, again, is getting harder all the time as the bar rises on customer expectations. Customer relationship management is an old-fashioned idea. At its heart is a systematic effort to put technology and processes in place to replicate, in some form or fashion, the intimacy of the interactions that once existed between the corner shopkeeper and his best customers.

With precision marketing, the objective is clear: to improve the efficiency and effectiveness by which a company can attract, retain, and leverage their most profitable customers. Efficiency means *doing things better*. In a corporate marketing context, it becomes a measure of how well marketing resources are utilized to achieve a particular goal. These goals can vary. Some of them—increasing website registration, for example, or improving in-store merchandizing—may result in no bump whatsoever in sales volume or profitability in the short term. Efficiency often translates into cost savings, which can become a particularly important consideration in a sluggish economy. In the first years of the new millennium, when companies everywhere were forced to cut staff and slow their spending, marketing organizations often made cost containment a number one priority.

Precision marketing seeks to reduce customer acquisition and support costs while improving the overall productivity of the marketing spend. In particular, this means minimizing the vast sums of money that go to waste by marketing to the wrong people. The wrong people are those who, for whatever reason, are simply poor candidates for buying the product or service at hand. As it is, companies throw away tens of millions of dollars each and every day hawking luxury cars to welfare recipients, tampons to men, lunch meats to vegetarians, credit cards to children, dog food to cat lovers, prescription eyeglasses to people with perfect vision, and so on. And each and every day, upon being subjected to a barrage of irrelevant marketing messages delivered to their homes courtesy of the mass media, millions of people share the same thought. It's one that can be best described by the Yiddish expression *loch in kop*, meaning "I need this [product or service] like a hole in the head."

In contrast to efficiency, effectiveness means *doing the right things.* It's a measure of the appropriateness of the goals chosen and the degree to which they are achieved, that is, redefining parts of the marketing process altogether, ultimately leading to new sources of revenues and profitability. Effectiveness often translates into strategic growth initiatives focused on using next-generation techniques to attract new customers or derive more value from existing customers. If efficiency means playing the same game better, then effectiveness might mean playing a slightly different game.

SEGMENTING FOR FUN AND PROFIT

The term *precision marketing* entered the business vernacular only recently. Yet many of the underlying concepts have a long history. The notion of *marketing demassification*, for example, originated with the futurist writer Alvin Toffler, who three decades ago foresaw a trend toward customized production and niche marketing. Other concepts date back to time immemorial. The notion of *customer intimacy*, for example, describes how business was conducted up until the modern period. Sellers and buyers talked to one another face-to-face, as we already discussed, and over time they naturally got to know one another. For a seller to recommend a particular item of merchandise to a buyer, based on his knowledge of that buyer's wants or needs, represents the earliest form of precision marketing.

Of course the law that causes gunpowder to explode is the same law that causes the sun to burn. In other words, precision marketing can take place on a small, unsophisticated scale, as we just illustrated. Or it can take place on a large, highly sophisticated scale, as will increasingly be the case going forward. The reasons we're so sure of this are threefold. First, the enabling technologies and analytical capabilities are rapidly adapting and evolving, simplifying the execution process while optimizing the business outcomes. Second, the competitive pressures in the marketplace are escalating and will continue to do so, whether in a good or bad economy. Third, the extent and magnitude of the tangible benefits tied to precision marketing are gaining recognition by a growing number of companies, across multiple industry sectors.

Precision marketing, in the large, highly sophisticated sun to burn sense, is fueled by a basic concept that nowadays we take for granted: *market segmentation*. The concept was first proposed half a century ago by an otherwise forgotten economist named Wendell Smith, who wrote that market segmentation represents a "precise adjustment of product or marketing effort to consumer or user requirements." According to Smith, this meant viewing "a heterogeneous market as a number of smaller homogeneous markets in response to differing product preferences among important market segments."[3]

31

The concept quickly took on a life of its own, winning the acclaim of other prominent market theorists, including a rising star at Harvard Business School named Theodore Levitt, who proceeded to take Smith's ideas a step further. Levitt wrote that markets are composed of individuals who often have different sets of wants and needs, and that markets should be segmented by these wants and needs rather than by product characteristics, as had long been the case. According to Levitt, major marketers should think of customers as "numerous small islands of distinctiveness."[4] By adjusting their marketing messages accordingly, companies could then increase the likelihood that each of the "small islands" would respond favorably to a purchase decision.

The idea of dividing up a large number of consumers into any number of smaller groups based on a set of common traits along one or more meaningful dimensions was radical thinking at the time. The idea of then targeting these various parcels of people with differentiated marketing messages was even more radical. Yet once the train had left the station, there was no stopping it. The 1960s produced an enormous proliferation of research articles on market segmentation, as one researcher after another tried his hand at proving—or disproving, as the case may have been—various correlations between consumer characteristics and buying behaviors. It didn't take long for the fervor, which had been mostly academic and theoretical in nature, to rise above the walls of the ivory tower and overflow into industry conferences and into the corporate boardrooms of companies intent on using strategic positioning as a means by which to create and sustain a competitive advantage.

Meanwhile, segmentation classifications evolved and expanded almost as quickly as researchers could test and validate their usefulness (Figure 1.1 highlights just a few of the key milestones in this evolution). At first, the classification schemes revolved around *demographics*, after researchers were able to gather enough compelling evidence to show that different groups of people tend to have different patterns of consumption, depend-

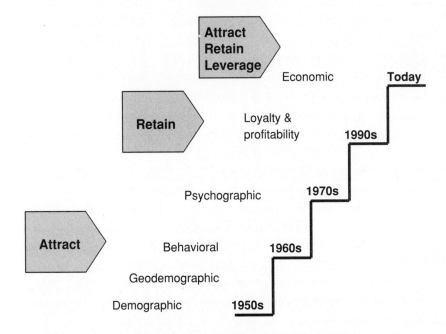

FIGURE 1.1   The Evolution of Market Segmentation

ing on such characteristics as occupation, race, and income level. *Geodemographics*, which takes demographics to the next level, by combining such variables as where a customer lives with home ownership and size of family, emerged shortly thereafter.

Next, the classifications expanded beyond the realm of easy-to-observe physical attributes tied to the U.S. Census, with *behavioral segmentation* joining the fray. Researchers had a field day, slicing and dicing consumer populations into previously unheard-of categories such as readiness to buy, motivation, and attitude. Later, in the 1970s, *psychographic* criteria such as personality and lifestyle characteristics also entered the mix, leading to a fresh wave of research fodder. An early study asked the question: Are the personalities of people who buy Fords discernibly different from those of people who buy Chevrolets? After collecting the data and tabulating the results, researchers were able to reach only one conclusion: *no.*

This example notwithstanding, psychographic segmentation has proven time and again to be a highly effective way to divide a population into various subsets, each with a "personality type" that speaks to that group's shared attitudes, outlooks, and levels of responsiveness to buying various products and services—and also, perhaps, the best ways for companies to market to them. Consider the seemingly generic population of Wealthy American Consumers. According to a recent survey by Harris Interactive, Wealthy American Consumers can, in fact, be divided into six distinct segments along psychographic dimensions, as follows: The Deal Masters, The Altruistic Achievers, The Secret Succeeders, The Status Chasers, The Satisfied Savers, and The Disengaged Inheritors. If it's a luxury car, diamond necklace, or designer gown that you're trying to sell, then peg your efforts toward targeting the Status Chasers, who covet showy displays of wealth, rather than the Disengaged Inheritors, who are loath to spend money on such nonessentials.

The intense state of theorizing, analyzing, and testing around market segmentation continued through the 1970s. By the early 1980s, however, researchers began to lose interest in the topic, probably because it seemed there were few stones left to turn. Whatever the reason, almost no notable contributions to the knowledge domain were made in the decade that followed. What research did take place amounted to a rehash of previous findings and variations on the same old themes. It wasn't until the mid-1990s that the dry spell finally ended.

That the topic once again found fertile ground was due to the emergence of a new set of segmenting criteria: *customer loyalty* and *profitability*. For the first time, the criteria were geared more toward *customer retention* than *customer acquisition*, and for good reason. "It costs a lot more to acquire a new customer than to retain an existing one," sang the choir of loyalty proponents. "Increasing your retention rate by a small amount can increase your profits by many times that amount." *Loyalty segmentation* represented a milestone in the annals of market segmentation, ultimately setting the stage for precision marketing.

Popularized by such notable authors as Fred Reichheld, Don Peppers, and Martha Rogers, the ideas that underlie loyalty segmentation are easy to understand (even if, for reasons that we get to later, operationalizing the process itself may be an altogether different matter). As the term suggests, loyalty segmentation means grouping customers according to their expected level of ongoing patronage. Executing this strategy means opening the hood on companies' integrated data repositories, to identify which customers are loyal *and* profitable—or are, at least, likely to become profitable in the future.

The profitability component is important, since loyalty does not always translate into profitability. "Loyalty for loyalty's sake isn't a goal," notes Marc Landsberg, head of corporate strategy at Paris-based Publicis Groupe, the world's fourth-largest communications company. "The economic question that every marketer is asking now is: 'What is the return on the cost of maintaining that loyalty?'"[5] It's a key part of the value equation, and one that the more vocal champions of loyalty segmentation have tended to overlook in the past.

Having identified the sets of loyal and also profitable customers, the next step would be to take whatever actions may be necessary to provide them with a disproportionate share of superior service, quality, and overall value. The goal is to become further ingratiated into their lives, and also into their bank accounts. By the same token, a company needs to determine which of its existing customers or customer segments are disloyal and unprofitable (and are likely to remain that way in the future, despite whatever intervention could possibly take place in an effort to make them profitable). Having completed the exercise, the company would need to find ways to minimize the cost of serving these customers. In some cases, this may even mean showing them to the door, in a process that we might simply refer to as "customer clearance."

Getting rid of people with negative relationship value is never a pleasant task, and it may seem to break the rules of social etiquette to part company with customers of any stripe. But then again, companies are in business for a specific reason: to generate value for employees and shareholders. Companies are under no obligation to play host to whatever riffraff happen to crash the party. The idea of purging bad customers, by making it cost prohibitive or otherwise difficult for them to do business with you, makes perfect economic sense (unless the company is government regulated, in which case it may be precluded from engaging in seemingly discriminatory practices). Certainly, the idea of purging bad customers helped advance our collective thinking about segmentation criteria, and about profit enhancement as a whole.

In summary, allocate resources *away* from low lifetime value customers and *toward* high lifetime value customers. These are, after all, people who arguably deserve to be rewarded for their ongoing patronage with higher priority service, complimentary upgrades, express lines, bonus points, and any number of other surprise-and-delight perks that ultimately make them feel special, important, and appreciated. Let it go to their heads. Why not? Of course, lavishing them with special care and attention can hardly qualify as a purely altruistic gesture given the obvious benefits the company stands to gain when it strengthens its relationships with high lifetime value customers. Ask the loyalty segmentation enthusiasts. They'll tell you that companies lose half their customers every five years, on average, but can double their profits by cutting that defection rate by a mere five percent. It's a compelling statistic, and reason enough to want to join the club.

With the advent of unified repositories for housing customer data, and improved analytical tools for gleaning actionable insights from that data, market segmentation is now set to advance to the next rung of the ladder: *economic segmentation*. As with loyalty segmentation, economic segmentation means using so-called *predictive analytics* to understand the long-term value of individual customers and customer segments. Importantly, the idea is then to apply that understanding to not only make decisions about differentiated customer service levels to existing customers based on their assumed lifetime value, but also to use the common characteristics of these customers as segmentation criteria for the purpose of marketing to future customers. In other words, to target "best-customer look-alikes." Economic segmentation takes the ideas of loyalty segmentation to the next level. By targeting customer prospects based on information about existing customers, it can be used not only to improve customer retention but also to drive customer attraction and leverage, and thus the overall marketing process.

We refer to the process of mapping the "genetic makeup" of desirable customer segments, based on an understanding of the common characteristics of existing customer segments, as *blueprinting the ideal customer*. A nice thing about "best-customer look-alikes" is that these prospects may be likely to respond to the same types of marketing messages that got their predecessors in the door. After all, if a company could identify a positive relationship between particular people and a particular marketing program, it could then assign other people with similar characteristics the same program—with some degree of confidence that what worked for the first group would also work for the second group.

Economic segmentation is a prerequisite for precision marketing. When combined with *response-based segmentation*—which, as we discuss in the next chapter, looks at people's response patterns with respect to their stated preferences, intentions, and mind sets—economic segmentation represents the next defining trend in the evolution of market segmentation. Moreover, we believe that it will take hold of and will shape the future of marketing as a whole.

WHERE MASS MARKETING HITS A BRICK WALL

While the terms *market segmentation* and *target marketing* are often used interchangeably, they are not the same. Marketing guru Philip Kotler, whose Foreword graces the first pages of this book, has long noted this distinction. He states that the process of target marketing entails three stages.

Market segmentation is the first stage, followed by *market targeting*, which involves selecting one or more of the customer segments previously identified. The third stage is *product positioning*, which means designing the so-called "marketing mix elements," including marketing communications, to fit the target segment. So, having identified the right segment and created the right marketing messages, the challenge is to deploy and/or exploit the right media vehicle. And therein lies the rub.

Generally speaking, the more narrow the target segment, the greater the challenge of finding a suitable media vehicle. And when it comes to driving volume sales increases in narrow customer segments, mass media vehicles like television, radio, billboards, magazines, and newspapers simply don't work all that well. Not surprisingly, most advertising sales executives would beg to differ.

Consider a special advertising supplement to the *New York Times*, published to coincide with the 2003–2004 upfront television programming season. On the cover, a stylized drawing depicts eight well-attired executives pushing their shopping carts up and down the aisles of a store, glancing at their checklists as they make their way from one end to the other. A sign is posted above each aisle. One sign reads: SINGLES. Another one reads: COUPLES 25–54. Other aisles are labeled FEMALES 30-PLUS, MALES 18–49, TEENS, KIDS, FAMILIES, and so on. The aisles are lined with shelves, all stacked from floor to ceiling with the same kind of merchandise: *eyeballs*. At the checkout line, the shoppers place their selections on a conveyer belt. A cashier rings up their purchases and places them into a paper bag, one eyeball at a time.

The illustration is clever and amusing, if more than a little deceptive. After all, to carry on the analogy, a shopper could select two eyeballs from the aisle labeled MALES 18–49, only to get home and discover that the eyeballs actually belong to a 12-year-old girl and a 60-year-old woman! The point is that, when buying mass media, marketers can never know exactly what they're going to get. They're bound to pick up a lot of nontarget eyeballs. More importantly, the category descriptions are bound to be so broad in scope as to be of little use in the first place. The experience is akin to visiting a grocery store with six aisles, each one labeled with a major food group: FRUITS, VEGETABLES, DAIRY, and so on. You select an item from the fruit aisle because you're craving an orange. But what you get may be an apple or a banana. For that matter, it may be a box of Fruit Loops.

By definition, mass marketing is an extremely crude tool for targeting population segments with characteristics more narrow than, say, a gender, an ethnicity, or a double-decade age range. Consider: A TV miniseries about Ronald Reagan may favor ads for Cadillac Devilles and Buick LeSabres, which have an average buyer age of 67, while a talk show featuring Snoop Dogg may favor ads for Volkswagen GTIs and Nissan Xterras, which have an average buyer age of 37. Yet *buyer age* may be only one of many factors that determine whether a consumer is likely to buy a Deville or a GTI. In fact, these aforementioned programs may attract viewers with a diversity of geodemographic, behavioral, and attitudinal characteristics, only some of which fit the patterns of those consumers likely to buy one of these cars.

Naturally, it would be much more effective to specifically target those viewers who fit the *multidimensional* profiles of a Deville or GTI owner—and who, moreover, have discretionary dollars to spend on a new car. It is wishful thinking to use broadcast TV as the marketing vehicle. Incidentally, Nielsen's income-range classifications are so wide that multibillionaires like Michael Dell and Bill Gates might be grouped into the same category as, say, a middle manager who can barely afford to buy a new Dell Dimension with Windows XP.

To put it another way, mass marketing is a sledgehammer as opposed to a drill. "At our company," one executive confided, "we call it 'spray-and-pray marketing.'" Remarked another executive: "There's plenty of evidence to show that we're spending more and more on mass marketing and getting less and less in return. There's also plenty of evidence to show that more targeted vehicles might be a better way to go."

Broadcast networks schedule programs that supposedly appeal to different customer segments at various, specific times of the day. But, again, to conclude that the programs attract a disproportionate number of people with the same multidimensional profiles as those in the target market, and that marketers can reach them in large numbers by slotting their 30-second commercial spots accordingly, often requires a big leap of faith. After all, what works well for Fisher-Price, eager to introduce its latest team of Rescue Heroes to Saturday morning cartoon aficionados, tends to fall apart for many other types of companies trying to play the matchmaking game among programs, products, and target audiences.

A few years ago, writing for the *New York Times Magazine*, author Michael Lewis (*Liar's Poker, Moneyball*) made the same basic point. Taking a scorchingly critical view of the entire TV advertising business, he argues that the basic formula for producing and selling TV programs has undergone practically no change whatsoever since the beginning of broadcast television—and, furthermore, that basic formula remains fundamentally flawed. He wrote:

> [T]he network that develops a new program assumes it can ensure its success by placing it in a desirable time slot, when a lot of people happen to be watching TV. It further assumes that it can pay for it by selling commercial time during that program. The commercials then get flung at whoever happens to be watching at the time. The entire history of commercial television suddenly appears to have been a Stalinist plot erected, as it has been, on force from above rather than choice from below. The networks have coerced, or attempted to coerce, consumers to watch programs and commercials in which they have no native interest. The advertisers who pay for the commercials have agreed to believe, without good evidence, that some meaningful percentage of viewers actually behave in this manner. They have further agreed to believe, again without good evidence, that the sort of people who watch a particular program have a more than ordinary interest in the products advertised on that program.[6]

Services like Simmons Market Research Bureau and Media-mark, in business to provide companies with audience composition data that guide their advertising–buying decisions, paint their reports only with the broadest of brush strokes. They have no other choice, given their limited powers of observation. Similarly, ratings from Nielsen Media Research are given based on different "universes" of viewers—breaking out, for example, how many women, Caucasians, or senior citizens watched a certain program. At best, all that a Nielsen rating can tell you is that, for example, 40 percent of the viewing audience between the ages of 18 and 34 with household incomes of more than $55,000 had their TVs tuned to a particular channel during a particular time period. It's not a whole lot of information to go on—although it's enough, apparently, to steer multimillion-dollar marketing investments.

In addition to the limitations in being able to measure audience granularity, one could argue that the data that does inform a Nielsen rating is somewhat dubious, given the viewership sample size (5,100 households, out of a total of 102 million). Even if the numbers could be assumed to be reasonably accurate in terms of representative sampling, as the statisticians would have us believe, the bigger question concerns what the ratings don't measure with respect to the qualitative factors that define *presence*.

What percentage of viewers use commercial breaks . . . to take a bathroom break? To engage in conversation? To get a bowl of ice cream? To walk the dog? To flip to a different channel?

Beyond physical presence, there's mental presence. Are viewers who are physically present even paying attention? Are they processing the information being presented to them, such that they might store it somewhere in the inner recesses of their memories and act upon it at some point in the future to make a purchase decision? Fact is, many people multitask while watching TV, sometimes engaging in half a dozen activities all at once. They check e-mails. They page through magazines. They chat on the phone. They pay their bills. They fold their laundry. Distractions are everywhere. In fact, media researchers use the term "the friends effect" to suggest that the more people there are in a room during a TV ad, the less likely each of them is to pay attention to it. How should these people get counted in terms of the rating system? By ascertaining what percentage of their cognitive energy was actually directed toward the TV screen? Maybe R&D engineers at Nielsen, tired of tinkering with their black boxes, are hard at work on some such device.

Cognitive Energy Reader Devices or not, what is certain about the future of broadcast TV advertising is that, over time, fewer viewers are likely to qualify as data points in the rating system. The universe is shrinking. This is especially true in light of the advent of digital video recorders (DVRs), along with newer types of set-top boxes with built-in DVR functionality now offered by cable providers. By allowing viewers to jump forward during playback by 30-second increments—or pause a live broadcast—these technologies make it a cinch to skip the commercials altogether. As such, they pose a serious threat to the $200 billion spent globally each year on traditional TV advertising.

Research studies suggest that TV viewers who subscribe to TiVo—the pioneering DVR brand—choose to skip about half of the commercials, on average. Multiply this percentage by the number of homes that may eventually come to own the machines—a number that, by some estimates, will reach 25 million by 2007—and it becomes clear that the impact will be a severe blow for advertisers in terms of lost viewership, not to mention the profound "Oz behind the curtain" spillover effect this could have on Nielsen-type metrics. It's an inevitability that many industry watchers readily acknowledge, and which has given rise to increased product placement within the actual programming, with brands now playing a supporting role, if not a starring role, on all kinds of TV shows.

Ironically, in 2003, TiVo unveiled a TV audience measurement system that reports the second-by-second viewing habits of its subscribers to advertisers. According to a company press release, the new service shows which commercials TiVo users actually watch in their entirety. Talk about precision? This is certainly a step in the right direction.

Now, imagine an even bigger—if decidedly more futuristic—step. It involves personalized technology that would allow a major marketer to transmit *different* ads to the same TV set depending on who in the house they believed was watching the programming at any given time. The behavior of the person running the remote control might dictate a certain profile, and that profile would swim back upstream. Or maybe the actual identity of the viewer could be determined—by using a "smart sofa," for example, such as one recently developed by scientists at Trinity College in Dublin, Ireland. On each leg of the sofa is a microchip sensor that identifies who is sitting down, based on the weight of that person. The ads that get served up would be tailored to that person's actual profile.

Until that day arrives, however, advertisers will have to contend with the general demographic appeal of the programming—which in many cases (e.g., news programs) is very general indeed. Therefore, the old adage "Put your money where the market is" works fine in the context of broadcast TV only so long as the parameters that are used to define the target market are extremely broad, the margin of error for reaching the audience is extremely large, and the possibility that the message might not actually get to a large portion of the audience is of no particular concern to the marketers who buy the traditional 30-second advertising spots.

Of course, broadcast TV isn't the only mass media channel available to marketers, and many companies have good reason to believe they can do better in terms of audience specificity by turning to so-called "niche media" vehicles. These vehicles include cable channels, newspapers, and consumer and business trade magazines. For example: Want to reach disproportionate numbers of young Hispanic American men? *No problemo.* Telemundo Network, a subsidiary of NBC, penetrates 91 percent of all Hispanic American TV households, and a large percentage of men are known to tune in during the 8 P.M. time slot.

Launched in 2003, Spike TV makes no apologies about its target audience: males 18–34 (as if this demographic was underserved by the existing broadcast and cable networks). Or maybe you want to reach stay-at-home moms in Middle America? Try WE, Oxygen, or Lifetime. With the tagline Television for Women, there's no mistaking Lifetime's target audience, as wide as it may be.

With more than 100 different channels available in most subscriber households, cable TV gives advertisers the ability to slice the pie thinner than ever, "micro-zoning" their messages at narrowly defined demographic and psychographic markets comprised of audiences with common characteristics or special interests. Michael Lewis, for one, believes that the secret to audience granularity lies in the convergence of cable TV and DVR functionality, noting in the aforementioned article that "the economics of targeted ads is so compelling that to make them possible is to make them certain."[7] Imagine a soccer channel that sells only soccer equipment. Or an acne channel that sells only skin care products. It's not hard to imagine, in fact, because such a reality already exists, if to a lesser degree. Consider the Eukanuba Tournament of Champions dog show on the Disney Network's Animal Planet cable channel. Not surprisingly, the program is interspersed with ads for Petco, IAMS dog food, and K9 Advantix mosquito treatment.

For their part, consumer magazines are commonly extolled to have the greatest market segmentation selectivity of any niche media type. In our view, however, the improvement is only incremental. While magazines certainly tend to be better than broadcast network TV—and even cable TV—at fracturing the mass audience into smaller pieces, the pieces are still a far cry from fulfilling the basic precepts that underlie precision marketing. Those precepts go well beyond the ability to reach target audiences by lifestyle and interests.

Consider *Men's Health*, a lifestyle magazine dedicated to showing men "the practical and positive actions that make their lives better," with articles covering fitness, relationships, nutrition, careers, grooming, travel, and health issues. The question: Does *Men's Health* know *your* fitness level, *your* marital status, *your* eating habits, *your* grooming behavior, how, when, and where *you* like to travel, or anything about *your* health? Like most other print magazines that show up in your mailbox, *Men's Health* may know only your mailing address and whether or not your subscription is paid up.

That said, magazine publishers have come to recognize that their greatest assets are their customer databases. "We should stop thinking of our database as just 'controlled subscribers,' and start thinking of it as 'registered information users,'" one publishing executive was quoted as saying, noting that he no longer describes his job as controlled circulation. "I explain that I leverage our company's free content to get users to register and give us permission to send them marketing messages."[8] Indeed, the future of online publications largely depends on how well these companies can collect the right customer data, and then glean insights from that data to serve up context-sensitive ads. That future is arriving quickly, judging from the number of online publishers already experimenting with various content-targeting and "online profiling" technologies designed to improve ad relevance—and, ultimately, convince marketers to spend more dollars on online advertising. (See pp. 49–51 for an overview of some of the emerging trends in online advertising.)

The routine collection of customer data conjures up the now-classic *New Yorker* cartoon shown in Figure 1.2. In the cartoon, the dog is thrilled at the anonymity the Internet affords him. If only it were true. Resourceful and creative marketers generally have the means at their disposal to collect an infinite amount of valuable information about their customers, both directly and indirectly, through a wide variety of means. (As an example, the customer database for Kraft Foods contains every household's name and address—110 million rows, in total—and *20 thousand facts* for every one of those households.) And if marketers know who a dog is and what makes him tick, then why not market to him in a context-sensitive manner? After all, they can infer, understand, and act upon the customer's context in a highly intelligent manner. Of course, marketers can also determine whether a

"On the Internet, nobody knows you're a dog."

FIGURE 1.2 The Dog Cartoon
© *The New Yorker.* Reprinted by permission.

customer is a dog in the sense of "an investment that produces a low return or a loss"—in which case, they may simply want to find that dog a new home.

In the next chapter, we explore several tactics marketers can employ in their efforts to capture data in reciprocal value exchanges with customers. For now, suffice it to say that magazines have a number of unique advantages in this area, by virtue of the natural offline-to-online synergies that exist. For them, it should be a relative cinch to get readers to register for a recipe, an e-mail newsletter, or a trial subscription. With increasing frequency, magazines are also using sweepstakes and contests as a draw. For its part, *Men's Health* recently sponsored a Win a Maserati Spyder for a Day! contest as a first step in capturing otherwise hard-to-get customer data. Now the magazine has a line of sight to delivering offers from "carefully selected third parties" that may be of greater relevance to its readers, based on their profile information.

Regardless of how the data is captured, or what combination of media vehicles is used to serve up the resultant marketing messages, precision marketing allows companies to move closer to achieving the Holy Grail of marketing: *delivering the right message to the right customer through the right channel at the right point in time.* Precision marketing assumes that people exist as more than two-dimensional cardboard cutouts that can be neatly sorted into various demographic, psychographic, and lifestyle buckets. Rather, it assumes that people are complex and unique entities who possess an enormous range of differing needs, desires, interests, behaviors, preferences, experiences, and other core characteristics, and that multidimensional descriptors are therefore required to do them justice. One-size-fits-all may work for terrycloth bathrobes that hang in the closets of the Ritz-Carlton hotel, but not for communicating marketing messages to differentiated audiences in ways that are meaningful and that ultimately lead to successful campaign results.

"Every data point helps you build a clearer picture of who your customers really are," says Mike Dobbs, vice president of product marketing at Cingular, the nation's second largest wireless carrier.[9] Today, the leading players in the wireless industry collect an enormous amount of data on their customers, beginning with cell phone usage. They know, for example, *where* a customer is using her phone, *how much* she's using it, *when* she's using it, whether she calls a large or small pool of numbers, whether the numbers are predominantly mobile or fixed-location, and so on. They know which features a customer likes, whether it's roadside assistance, text messaging, photo sharing, info alerts, or sports score updates. They know if a customer has a family plan, such as a primary line and two secondary lines for kids. And when a customer makes a call into customer service, they know the nature of the call.

Imagine how much more powerful this data collection becomes if the company can then marry it with various external data sources. Suddenly, the company also knows a customer's age and education, where she shops, which magazines she reads, which cars she buys, and so on. Now it can paint a multidimensional picture of each customer.

Contrast this picture with a typical mass market audience stratification, which might be simply described as *Females 18–35 who earn between $30K and $50K a year.* It's an incredibly broad spectrum, when the *real* audience might reside at a far more granular and multifaceted level. For example: *Females 18–25 who earn between $40K and $50K a year, belong to a health club, drink Diet Coke, order books online, rent romantic comedies, own a dog, floss regularly, have outstanding student loans, occasionally respond to e-mail promotions from familiar brands, own a Dell Axim handheld with Wi-Fi connectivity, dine out at least twice a week, and use a rinse aid in their dishwashers.* Can marketers possibly reach this target market with any degree of accuracy without, at the same time, wasting money reaching large numbers of people who don't fit the bill? It would have been a pipe dream just a few years ago. But in the age of precision marketing, it may simply depend on the depth and breadth of the customer database, and the ability to manage the data in ways that yield meaningful outcomes. Like the *X-Files* motto, the data is actually "out there" somewhere. And where there is data there will follow marketers wielding new technology solutions.

CONTEXTUAL ADVERTISING: COMING SOON TO A WEB PAGE NEAR YOU

Conventional banner ads, whether confined to a rectangular box or set free to roam for a few seconds across the screen, trampling over any articles that cross their paths, are little different from their old media counterparts. In many ways, the ads are analogous to those that show up along the highway, surround a print magazine article, or partition your favorite sitcom. The ads are interruptive, or at least somewhat intrusive. They take people away from what they are doing to try to sell them mostly random products and services.

Enlightened marketers know that if content is king, as Internet pundits like to say, then context is emperor. It's the underlying premise of this book. And it's the reason that many advertisers see such enormous promise in the recent growth of online services that can link their marketing messages to website content in a far more targeted and context-sensitive manner. In effect, these services can turn random ads into relevant ads. After several false starts, precision marketing on the Web is finally coming to life, if only in a nascent form.

Two Internet stars—Google and Overture (now part of Yahoo!)—are leading the way, by offering services that respond to keyword searches with paid text ads. For example, type the word "dog food" into Google or one of its content partner sites, and the search results pages will feature a series of "sponsored links" from any number of pet supply companies vying for your business. "It's the Yellow

Pages, classifieds, and direct mail rolled into a single just-in-time pitch," noted one commentator.*

In 2003, Google and Overture took the concept to the next logical step, unveiling content-targeting services that allow paid text links to move beyond the search results pages. For the first time, the links can also appear adjacent to relevant website content in place of those often-random banner ads. For example, an article about tourism in Barcelona might be accompanied by links to companies that offer airline tickets, car rentals, and travel guide books about Spain. The ability to serve up relevant ads based on the specific content of an article represents a huge advance in terms of precision marketing.

Another recent innovation allows publishers to dynamically insert relevant links within the actual body of the text. According to sources at Google, the technology can automatically "crawl" through the text and "understand" its meaning—then, from a customer base that numbered more than 100,000 advertisers in 2003, create links to related ads. "The advertising needs to be highly relevant to the content of the page," notes Tim Armstrong, vice president of marketing. "When you look at it from that standpoint, the advertising starts to become very valuable."†

Can search engines, not to mention online publishers, mingle content with ads without muddying the waters of objectivity? Armstrong argues that Google has a strong policy on church and state, by ensuring that all ads are clearly marked as such. He adds that the advertising programs are built around trust. "We want users to trust us for unbiased information and advertisers to trust us for contextual placements," he says.‡

What's next for Google, Overture, and other technology providers that enable this form of precision marketing on the Web? In our view, several key advances will take place over the next few years. First, the "sponsored links" section will move beyond text-only ads to also incorporate streaming, interactive media. Second, the targeted ads on publisher sites will take into account not only the

---

*John Battelle, "Putting Online Ads in Context," *Business 2.0*, June 2003.
†Interview with Tim Armstrong by Jeff Zabin, July 8, 2003.
‡Ibid.

context of the article, but also the characteristics of the readership, as well as the subsegments within it—to the point of serving up different ads to different readers. For example, a Honda ad linked to an article about cross-country road trips might present an Odyssey to a young family but an S2000 to a retired executive.

Third, the ads will become untethered from the corresponding articles. After all, a reader who has finished reading the article about road trips and has now moved on to another article may still be interested in viewing the Honda ads. "Online profiling" technologies are already being used by some online publishers—including the Wall Street Journal Online, which deploys a system developed by Revenue Science. The system classifies users based on their clickstreams. For example, a reader who visits the technology section five days in a row is automatically added to a Technology Enthusiast category. As a member of the category, the reader may now be exposed to a disproportionate number of technology-related ads, no matter where on the site they decide to venture. Other categories include Car Buffs, Health Enthusiasts, and Mutual Fund Aficionados.

Finally, geographic segmentation will become a major factor. It will influence paid search results—as well, eventually, as the ads that appear on publisher sites. Based on user IP addresses, query topics, and/or response-based data (e.g., a Zip code), the search results could present location-based advertising as yet another layer of contextualization. Type "Omaha plumbers" into Google, for example, and behold a list of local plumbers. Why stop there? The list could include anything Omaha-related—Borsheim's Jewelers, La Casa restaurant, the Joslyn Art Museum. And that aforementioned Honda ad? Now it might feature information about Omaha dealerships where the user could go to test-drive a new Odyssey—or an S2000, as the case may be.

THE POWER OF COMPLEMENTARITY

By definition, traditional media are mass marketing vehicles, and will continue to function as such until true interactivity and technology converge to fundamentally redefine the nature of the beast. Michael Lewis' unbridled enthusiasm for the possibilities of digital recording makes for some compelling reading. But it ultimately misses the mark in the context of the current discussion, for one simple reason: You can't turn a mass marketing vehicle into a precision marketing vehicle any more than you can turn an airplane into a rocket ship. Nor, really, is there any reason to even try. The two types of vehicles were designed to different specifications. They have different features and perform different functions.

Yes, great power comes from knowing who your customers are at a granular level, and being able to serve up customized offers that are sure to resonate with their specific wants and needs. By the same token, great power comes from being able to reach very large groups of people—perhaps tens of millions of them en masse, in the case of, say, a Super Bowl blimp—with a marketing message that may, in fact, be relevant for a significantly large portion of them. If awareness is your goal, it's hard to beat a giant blimp hovering over a world-class sporting event. But if winning new customers and making an incremental jump in sales is your goal, blimps may be little more than dressed-up hot air.

So, traditional mass marketing is not dying, as some pundits have prognosticated—not by a long shot. Still, for reasons that we've suggested, some smart marketers are beginning to question the wisdom of placing *all* of their bets on mass marketing vehicles. Increasingly, they are asking themselves an old question, which inspires a new set of possibilities: Do we cast a wide net in an effort to catch as many fish as possible or do we cast a narrow net in an effort to catch only the biggest fish? In most cases, the right answer is: *We do both.* The reason becomes apparent when you stop to reflect on some of the historic analogs of technology innovation.

For starters, consider the forebear of the DVR—the VCR, which first began to make inroads into people's homes in the early 1980s. For studio executives, believing that audiences would no longer flock to movie theaters but would instead bring the silver screen into their homes, the VCR was cause for alarm. Would video rentals cannibalize ticket sales? In fact, as we all know, the number of movie theaters has more than doubled over the past two decades. In 2003, movie theaters were expected to generate roughly $20 billion in revenues—a number roughly equal to the video and DVD rental market. Rather than render the movie theater business obsolete, the VCR created a new market that *complemented* it, by giving customers alternative viewing occasions.

Our friend and sometime collaborator Mohan Sawhney has aptly dubbed this phenomenon "the myth of substitution."[10] The idea is that new technologies often turn out to be complements, not substitutes, to the old technologies that they were envisaged to replace. Consider the rise of television. Some pundits were convinced that TV sets would reduce radio consoles to firewood. But again, these naysayers failed to grasp the complementary nature of the two technologies. True, radio consoles slowly disappeared as a living room centerpiece. Yet radio itself continues to thrive to this day, thanks largely to the rush hour commute. It simply serves a different need than it did previously, and in a different situation. (Decades earlier, when the radio first came into vogue, Henry Steinway had been advised by many that he might as well shut down his piano-making factories. Henry wisely ignored this expert advice.)

How about the microwave oven? Originally positioned as a substitute for the conventional oven, it instead *joined* the conventional oven in the category of "indispensable kitchen appliances." Analog watches and digital watches. Standard incandescent light bulbs and halogen light bulbs. Landline phones and cell phones. As the curtain opens on a new technology, the old technology doesn't necessarily follow its cue to exit stage left. Instead, quite often it remains in the limelight, and for good reason. The new and the old co-exist in a hybrid world where each performs a distinct but equally valuable function.

Now think about the "myth of substitution" in the context of mass marketing and precision marketing. As the long-reigning approach to driving incremental sales revenue and overall brand awareness, mass marketing correlates to the old technology. Precision marketing, on the other hand, is the new technology. And indeed, as we've suggested, the advent of precision marketing was predicated on the convergence of several new technologies, from data mining and campaign response tools to applications that enable new degrees of freedom around customer profile management, thus allowing companies to customize their messages to fit the needs and desires of narrow customer segments. In general, the more narrow the segment, the more customizable the message—and the better the opportunity to elicit an actionable response that ultimately translates into a positive business outcome.

Taken to an extreme, that is, a customer segment of *one*—precision marketing bears a striking resemblance to one-to-one marketing, that idealistic (but, again, usually impractical) notion of achieving customer intimacy that we mentioned earlier in this chapter. Championed over the past decade by Peppers and Rogers in their series of bestselling books, the idea is simple, at least as they explain it: *Rather than mass marketing a particular product or service to a large group of customers, companies can target specific customers to determine and then meet their individual needs.* Many others, including the president of an ACNielsen research subsidiary, have since echoed this same view—that is, "Technological advancements are rapidly enabling a new form of marketing—one-to-one marketing—that will replace mass marketing."[11] But to suggest that companies abandon their mass marketing efforts in favor of targeting only specific customers presents a false dichotomy.

Today the question that most large companies face is not Should I embrace mass marketing *or* precision marketing? but How can I combine the two approaches to achieve the desired objectives? It's not an either/or proposition, and rarely will the right answer lie with only one approach. Therefore, the real decision becomes one of appropriate resource allocation. Just as companies need to determine the right marketing mix in terms of channels, prices, and so on, so, too, do they need to determine the right mix between mass marketing and precision marketing.

Cingular, for one, is very mindful of the need to strike this balance. According to Mike Dobbs, the company utilizes mass marketing on a national scale to communicate "some differentiated element about Cingular that the mass market would want to know about." But in order to be more effective in telling customers "how the company is truly different, and in communicating the 'so what?'" in the context of these customers' specific needs, Cingular resolved to take a far more segmented approach, using precision marketing techniques. The decision meant a radical upgrade of its database and analytics capabilities, which the company undertook in 2002. Clearly, these multimillion dollar investments were made out of competitive necessity. With half a dozen or more major players now competing in all of the markets where Cingular has put its stake in the ground, Dobbs notes that the company's ability to increase market share "requires much more targeted messaging to the right customer segments."[12]

Or consider SBC Communications, a Fortune 30 company that owns a 60 percent stake in Cingular. In April 2003, SBC rolled out a mass marketing campaign to promote its all-you-can-eat-local-and-long-distance-for-one-low-price package. The company chose not to target-market the offer, believing it would have wide appeal across practically all customer segments. SBC did, however, decide to measure the "take rates"—that is, the response and sales measures—by predefined segments, and to try to understand the dynamics of these take rates at the channel level. By applying additional intelligence, SBC hoped to gain insights into how it could further stimulate the package on a more targeted basis to increase customer share of wallet. So again, the idea was to drive initial interest through mass marketing, then upsell other products and services, such as wireless and DSL, through precision marketing.

So long as Cingular, SBC, and hundreds of other companies have faith that mass marketing vehicles can accomplish at least some portion of their overall marketing objectives, broadcast television, as well as radio, magazines, and newspapers, will continue to account for well over half of the $250 billion that Corporate America spends each year on advertising. Today that faith appears to be stronger than ever, judging by the fact that ad agencies, on behalf of their clients, spent a record $9 billion to buy commercial time on the broadcast networks ahead of the 2003–2004 prime time season.

At the same time, given the need to also reach homogeneous audiences with highly relevant messages delivered in the context of their specific needs, precision marketing promises to play an instrumental role in the eternal quest to increase customer profitability and improve Marketing ROI (corporate goals that today top the agenda of practically every CEO). Again, there's no contradiction. The two approaches go hand in hand. They should work in tandem, each one doing what it does best, toward achieving the common goal. Often, this will mean finding creative ways to exploit the synergies—by conducting offline-to-online promotions in a mass marketing campaign to capture customer information that can be subsequently used in a precision marketing campaign, for example, as we discuss in Chapter 2. Going forward, the real visionaries will be those who capitalize on the myriad ways in which mass marketing and precision marketing complement one another. For inspiration, they need look no further than their VCRs.

MARKETING IN A WORLD OF "PREDICTABLE IMBALANCE"

In terms of their economic impact on corporate revenues and profitability, some customers matter a whole lot more than others. It's an irrefutable fact, one of the most basic facets of marketing, and part of the logic that underlies virtually any segmentation strategy. It's true not only for big ticket items—consider: the highest earning fifth of the population accounts for 55 percent of new car sales volume, up from 40 percent in 1980—but across most any goods and services sold in the marketplace today. While the exact figures and percentages may vary somewhat, depending on the industry context and also on whom you ask, everyone agrees that a relatively small number of customers tend to account for a disproportionate amount of a brand's current value, as well as its future growth potential.

Consider Procter & Gamble, the largest U.S. maker of household products and a paragon of mass marketing. The company routinely spends more than $2 billion each year on advertising and promotions in the United States, and more than $3.5 billion worldwide. But is P&G *really* a mass market brand company? It sure looks like one, at least on the surface, given that it's home to such blockbuster brands as Crest toothpaste, Puffs tissues, and Tide detergent. After all, what customer segments *don't* brush their teeth, blow their noses, and wash their laundry? Today P&G can easily boast of having some assortment of bottles, cans, rolls, cartons, boxes, and canisters on the shelves, under the sinks, and in the closets of more than 95 percent of all U.S. households.

The brand ubiquity of P&G is downright staggering. Global business units compete in product categories with more than 75 percent household penetration. Individual brands compete in product categories with more than 35 percent household penetration. With total sales of more than $40 billion worldwide in 2002, and nearly 300 brands under its roof, P&G stands as the global leader in 7 of the 12 different product categories in which it competes. Given the company's sheer magnitude, one could easily reach the conclusion that P&G is a mass market brand company. Indeed, one would be hard-pressed to reach any other conclusion.

Upon closer examination, however, the numbers tell a slightly different story. For P&G and for Unilever, Kraft, ConAgra, and probably every other leading consumer packaged-goods company, the so-called "valuation skew"—that is, the degree to which the value of a customer base is concentrated in a small percentage of customers—is extremely steep, meaning that a small percentage of customers accounts for the majority of the value of the customer base. This phenomenon is often referred to as The 80:20 Rule or The Pareto Law, after the Italian economist Vilfredo Pareto. Based on his studies of global wealth distribution, Pareto made the observation that "a minority of input produces the majority of results." Certainly, the concept—what Pareto himself called "predictable imbalance"—is highly applicable in the context of customer value contribution. In the case of P&G, less than 7 percent of all households, on average, account for more than 60 percent of the company's brand sales and 70 percent of its profit. In other words, 93 percent of all households are responsible for less than 30 percent of the profit that a typical P&G brand generates.

This fact conjures up yet another old marketing adage: I know half my advertising dollars are wasted; I just don't know which half! The adage paints an overly optimistic picture, as most brand managers wish that *only* half of their advertising dollars were wasted. The reality of the situation is that, on any particular day, perhaps upwards of 90 percent of a company's marketing dollars are wasted. Consider some brand examples from P&G. In the case of Pantene, the bestselling haircare brand in the world, approximately 5 percent of households drive 60 percent of sales and 70 percent of profit. For Tide detergent, a market leader for nearly 55 years, approximately 10 percent of households drive 60 percent of sales and 70 percent of profit. How about Pringles potato chips? While just about everyone enjoys the stackable crunch, it turns out that not everyone buys Pringles in quantities that make for a good customer, with approximately 12 percent of households driving 60 percent of sales and 70 percent of profit.

Not surprisingly, the bull's-eye for a brand like Metamucil, a fiber-therapy laxative, is much smaller. In a recent TV ad, a park ranger stands next to Old Faithful and explains that for thousands of years the geyser has been "well, faithful." A tourist asks,

"What causes it to stay so regular?" The answer comes in the next scene, when the park ranger pours a glass of Metamucil into the geyser hole. In 2003, the advertisement aired on prime time network TV—even with just over 1 percent of households driving 60 percent of sales and 70 percent of profit. In light of its niche market appeal (primarily for older people, who are most likely to suffer from constipation), should Metamucil really be treated as a mass market brand? The rationale for doing so is questionable, unless the purveyors of P&G customer insight have reason to believe that fiber-therapy laxatives are set to become the next big health craze.

Metamucil claims: *All fiber is not created equal.* Clearly, what is true of fiber is also true of customers, as we have already shown. In fact, across all of P&G's brands, less than three percent of households are thought to offer the greatest new growth potential. Needless to say, three percent does not equal a mass market population. With a small fraction of households driving a disproportionate amount of revenues and new growth potential, it would seem to only make sense that P&G earmark some portion of its marketing budget toward facilitating more personalized interactions with the customers who account for the vast majority of its business. And lo and behold, that's exactly what P&G is doing, with ever-higher levels of active experimentation.

This follows recent pronouncements by CEO A.G. Lafley and Global Marketing Officer Jim Stengel that the company must do a better job of pinpointing its high-value customers (what it refers to as "prime prospects") with targeted marketing messages—and, furthermore, that it must do a better job of assessing, tracking, and reporting the ROI for all marketing expenditures. Both agendas are now regarded as corporate mandates within the P&G organization, and as promises to shareholders that the company will utilize its formidable marketing engine more aggressively—and more intelligently—to generate higher returns.

GETTING POINTS FOR CONTEXT SENSITIVITY

Customer loyalty is on the decline. Markets are becoming increasingly fragmented. CEOs are demanding higher levels of marketing effectiveness. At the same time, a corporate edict exists within many companies that prevents the marketing organization from increasing its spending to compensate for the loss in customer loyalty, not to mention the increased challenges wrought by the competitive environment. Instead, the organization is expected to spend roughly the same amount of money that it has always spent on a marketing basis per profit point. Unable to escape the fixed marketing-spend-to-profitability ratio, the challenge becomes one of needing to wring more profit out of the same amount of marketing dollars.

Is mass marketing the best way to meet this challenge? Some old-line executives continue to think so, perhaps only because it's hard for them to imagine a world of better alternatives. In making his case, one executive compared mass advertising to a game of roulette. In roulette, he explained, there are black rows and red rows, and gamblers can place bets anywhere they please. From the gamblers' viewpoint, the odds of winning seem fairly reasonable. But the fact of the matter is that, given enough time, the casino always wins. The reason, of course, is that the casino has a very subtle edge that tips the odds in its favor: a green zero chip and a green double-zero chip. So the odds really aren't 50-50, as they may at first appear. On a double-zero roulette table, the house advantage is actually 5.26 percent. "Mass marketing does the same thing for our brand," the executive continued. "Everybody knows about our brand, but a continuous stream of gentle reminders keeps it top of mind."

Is marketing about producing a continuous stream of gentle reminders that reach a lot of people with a lot of frequency over a long period of time? In some cases, the answer is *yes*. Mass marketing will keep its place as a cornerstone of brand communication, as we suggested, until the convergence of new technologies and changing viewer behavior eventually forces it to change. Meanwhile, it seems to us that companies should not want to resign themselves to accepting a house advantage that consists of the corporate equivalent of two green casino chips. Given the new degrees of freedom around the use of customer data for creating targeted marketing campaigns, many companies are now able to get a lot more bang for the buck. By using precision marketing to supplement their mass marketing efforts, they can create what, in effect, amounts to an unfair advantage.

Again, that unfair advantage comes, first and foremost, from learning as much as possible about the key attributes of their prime prospects, that is, customers who contribute the greatest amount of value to the business. That knowledge has been traditionally captured through focus groups but can be more easily garnered through precision marketing programs, as we explain. The knowledge translates into customer insights, which, in turn, inform the creation and delivery of targeted marketing messages.

Consider an example from Kraft Foods, where the overall marketing strategy has undergone dramatic change in recent years. Instead of aiming for a general target in terms of customer prospects, brand managers and media planners are now instructed to aim for a bull's-eye, and to shift more of their marketing funds in support of the effort to hit that bull's-eye. "It feels uncomfortable when you first start marketing that way because you're putting all this money toward reaching a very small group," explained one brand manager. "But without this very small group, you wouldn't be in business." For dressings and other "pourables," the bull's-eye is the Salad Lover. The Salad Lover, by definition, is someone who eats salads two or three times a day. For them, it's all about the taste. The dressing makes the salad. Eating a salad without the right kind of dressing would be a cardinal sin in their book. For Kraft, the challenge is to discern the most effective message for the Salad Lover. Mind you, it's a very different message from the one Kraft would want to communicate to someone simply looking to prepare a side salad with dinner.

Marketing to an attractive subsegment of the market in a contextualized manner is what precision marketing is all about. At the same time, the approach flies in the face of the traditional, industry-standard metrics for quantifying advertising exposure, and thereby calculating advertising effectiveness. With most mass media, advertisers seek to reach a percentage of a set audience at a specific number of times, measured in terms of *reach* and *frequency*. Online ad sellers, as well as ad-serving companies, are currently negotiating standards that correlate to these same units of measurement for Web-based advertising—in other words, doing their best to conform to a deeply flawed model.

Reach is defined as the percentage of people within a given "universe" who are exposed to a particular advertisement at least once within a given period of time (the *frequency*). The universe is typically based on total U.S. households—in other words, just about any American citizen with a heartbeat. Gross ratings points (GRPs) are calculated by dividing the gross impressions of a media buy by the population of the audience reached, without making any allowances for the relevance of that audience. The equation assumes that all people are equal in terms of customer value—which, as we've said, couldn't be further from the truth. After all, reaching one right person is better than reaching a million wrong people. So, again, while media buyers try their best to secure advertising time on networks, programs, and dayparts that are likely to attract disproportionate shares of the target audience (however broad buyers' interpretations of the word *target* may be), their degree of success in accomplishing this goal is reflected nowhere in the GRPs.

To remedy the situation, and in light of the host of new possibilities around precision marketing, we propose the integration of a new metric: *context sensitivity*. We believe that context sensitivity points (CSPs), calculated using a scale that relies on both implicit and explicit data to measure the extent to which the offer actually fits the wants, needs, and interests of the target audience, could eventually evolve into a bona fide metric. Media planners could use it, for example, as an overlay to their standard set of metrics for evaluating a media buy. For them, the familiar choice between reach and frequency has always been one of trying to decide whether it's better to reach fewer people more times or more people fewer times with the marketing message. The use of CSPs would change the equation, particularly in terms of reach, to reflect the "relevancy makeup" of the audience, as the overriding mentality shifts from "the more the merrier" to "quality over quantity."

Context is commonly defined as that which surrounds, and gives meaning to, something else. Context can transform ambiguity into exactly the right information. So essential is context processing to the human mental function that researchers have linked its impairment to cognitive problems related to aging and schizophrenia. In software applications, context-sensitive help provides information related to the particular feature that you're using. Context-sensitive marketing means presenting people with offers that are relevant to their particular needs, interests, and situations. Think of it as *just-in-time marketing* as opposed to *just-in-case marketing*. Mass marketing embodies just-in-case marketing. TV ads that people don't watch, junk mail that people don't read, and newspaper circulars that line the kitty litter box are common manifestations of just-in-case marketing.

TURNING CUSTOMERS INTO "CLUB MEMBERS"

In the 1977 Oscar-winning movie *Annie Hall*, Woody Allen plays Alvy Singer, a neurotic comedy writer. The movie opens with a monologue in which Alvy remarks that an important joke for him is one usually attributed to Groucho Marx, but that appears originally in Freud's wit and its relation to the unconscious. "I would never wanna belong to any club that would have someone like me for a member," he says.

"Clubs" and "members" can be a useful way to think of customer segments and individual customers, respectively. From the perspective of a company that engages solely in mass marketing, *everyone*—including Woody Allen—is a member of the same club. That club is called All Consumers. In reality, everyone also belongs to any number of other clubs, perhaps millions of them. These smaller, more exclusive clubs require longer descriptive names to do them justice. The Generation-Y-Females-with-a-Propensity-to-Respond-to-Online-Promotions-for-Student-Loan-Consolidation Club, for example, or The Married-Golf-Playing-Text-Messaging-Business-Executives-with-Young-Children-Currently-Planning-a-Family-Vacation Club. Some descriptive names may run an entire page. In any case, the nice thing about these clubs is that neither their descriptive names nor their membership rosters are set in stone. New clubs can be dynamically generated on an ad hoc basis whenever the need arises.

This capability can make all the difference in the world in terms of marketing response rates, given the ability to send differentiated, context-sensitive messages. Recently, we architected a precision marketing program for a bank that has a large number of renters as clients, which may correlate with their likelihood to become first-time house buyers. Culling profile information from the bank's customer database, we generated a Young Renters Club. We asked the members of that club if they would like to receive e-mails. We sent e-mails to a total of 6,100 registrants; 4,500 of them opted in to receive our club newsletter e-mails. Of that 4,500, the average open rate for the 7 e-mails we sent was 80 percent. Of those who opened the e-mails, eight percent booked mortgages during the three-month period that we ran the campaign. Obviously, the campaign would never have succeeded without the ability to actualize this notion of clubs and members.

Call it database marketing, differential marketing, prime prospect marketing, target marketing, or any one of the half dozen or so other terms that people have been batting around for the past few years to describe various aspects of the same basic concept. The important point is that precision marketing has now arrived in full force. Today, transaction and interaction databases can be unified across all parts of the extended business network and mined in real time, with adaptive offers presented to customers based on their personal profiles. Marketing optimization algorithms can determine the best possible match among offers, customers, and channels. The possibilities for improving the outcomes of practically any given marketing program are virtually endless.

Yet no matter how futuristic the world of precision marketing may seem, behind the scenes is a basic three-step process:

1. Capture and manage customer data
2. Analyze the data to derive strategic insights
3. Use the insights to drive more efficient and profitable customer interactions

The process brings to mind another *New Yorker* cartoon, this one published a decade after the one about the two dogs and the computer. The cartoon depicts a mother bird and her baby birds all perched on a limb. Below them, a businessman, sitting on a park bench, is reading the newspaper. "Today's lesson is about targets of opportunity," declares the mother bird.

"Targets of opportunity" captures the very essence of precision marketing. And "context" is what differentiates a valuable offer from everyday bird poop.

2
THE PRECISION
MARKETING CYCLE

Many will pass through and knowledge will be increased.

—The Book of Daniel, reproduced (in Latin) on
the title page of Francis Bacon's *Instauratio Magna*

Sir Francis Bacon, the Renaissance-era statesman, essayist, and philosopher, secured his place in history by introducing the so-called "scientific method." He described it as the development of a hypothesis, the design of experiments to test it, the analysis of the results, and the subsequent rethinking of the original thesis. He viewed the method as "a light that would eventually disclose and bring into sight all that is most hidden and secret in the universe." And indeed, over the next four centuries, Bacon's approach to scientific thought would serve to deepen human understanding across every possible area of scientific investigation.

W. Edwards Deming, a physicist who became a celebrated professor of statistics and an influential force in the meteoric rise of Japanese industry after World War II, was among the first to embrace the basic tenets of the scientific method in the context of business management. With respect to industrial operations, Deming argued that companies could achieve better quality control by recording the number of product defects, analyzing why they happened, instituting changes, recording how much quality improved, and then refining the process. At the time, Deming's statistical process-control-based management approach was nothing short of revolutionary. It unleashed new degrees of productivity that ultimately helped to create a wide competitive gap between U.S. and Japanese manufacturing efficiency, much to the chagrin of American automobile and steelworker unions.

Half a century has passed since Deming's groundbreaking work made a big splash (at least in the waters off the Pacific Rim) within the realm of quality control. Today, the scientific method—now commonly known as the Plan-Do-Check-Act cycle—is promising to have an equally profound effect within the realm of marketing management. With the advent of new technology platforms, new cross-channel integration tools, and new degrees of analytical rigor around customer data, a growing number of companies are already embracing Plan-Do-Check-Act as a way to improve the overall productivity of their marketing investments.

We call this modified version of the Plan-Do-Check-Act cycle the *Precision Marketing Cycle.* It consists of a closed-loop process predicated on the science of customer data analytics and fueled by the belief that marketing effectiveness *must* be measured.

The Precision Marketing Cycle presents a conceptual framework for planning and implementing precision marketing programs and for managing, measuring, and forecasting Marketing ROI. Before we get to describing the four stages of the framework, however, it's important to lay out the reasons for the mounting pressure that marketing organizations today face and the variety of ways in which they are responding to that pressure. It's also important to understand why the call for measurement and accountability presents such a significant challenge for so many of them.

GETTING SERIOUS ABOUT MARKETING ROI

In the fall of 2002, the corporate sponsors of the Marketing Science Institute (MSI), an organization of marketing leaders from the business and academic communities, voted on what they believed should be the highest priority topic for academic study over the following two years. The topic that won, hands down, was "Assessing Marketing Productivity (Return on Marketing) and Marketing Metrics." In summing up the reasons for the choice, the MSI noted that "the pressure to demonstrate marketing effectiveness has never been greater."

These same sentiments were echoed a year later at the Association of National Advertisers' 93d annual conference, where the agenda revolved around such topics as return on investment for ad spending and the need to determine marketing accountability. The challenge is "bringing science to the art of marketing," declared Robert Liodice, president of the association, noting that companies today need to focus on "squeezing every ounce of value from every dollar of their marketing spend."

For its part, in announcing its topic selection, the MSI suggested that assessing the impact of marketing investments requires access to the right set of tools—implying that such tools have yet to land on most marketers' workbenches. Fact is, until recently, attitudinal measures such as focus group surveys were essentially the *only* tools most marketers could use to gauge campaign effectiveness prior to launch. And for assessing the outcomes of these same campaigns after the fact? Generally speaking, marketers could use only incremental sales data (usually, hopelessly incomplete) from syndicated reseller channels, with perhaps an occasional brand awareness study thrown in for good measure (no pun intended). In short, the measurement process could hardly be called scientific.

Moreover, marketing expenditures have often been rationalized on the basis of vague propositions like "We're building long-term awareness, consideration, and latent brand value." Sounds like a worthy goal. Yet such propositions can be hard to test, especially in the short term. That's beside the fact that brand awareness does not necessarily translate into a purchase decision. Nobody can say for sure that a specific percentage change in awareness will invariably lead to a specific percentage change in revenue. Consider McDonald's global marketing efforts, which today total more than $1 billion. You may know everything McDonald's wants you to know about its food, prices, service, convenience, ambiance, cleanliness, and latest line of movie tie-in toys. McDonald's may, in fact, be "top of mind" when you think of fast food. Still, for whatever reason, you may never set foot in any one of its 30,000 restaurants. McDonald's could spend a fortune to further increase your awareness, to the point that the ads are playing in your head day and night, and could still get absolutely nothing in return, simply because awareness does not always equal action.

Unfortunately, using actual sales data as the primary performance metric of a mass marketing campaign is also problematic. Why? Because when it comes to gauging performance, the correlation between cause and effect tends to be nonlinear, and, therefore, somewhat nebulous. Consider the difficulty of measuring the response to an individual ad exposure. Trouble is, an exposure may be part of a larger "momentum effect"—or what industry insiders refer to as *adstock*. The idea is that the impact of a single ad, or even an ongoing campaign, becomes part of a cumulative process that pays off at some point in the future after having reached a certain saturation point in the mind of the consumer. Such long-term value accumulation, assuming it actually happens in some form or other, defies short-term yardsticks.

Also, at times, it can be hard to know whether a jump in sales volume was the result of a newly launched marketing campaign that really bowled people over—creating a sense of urgency to zip out and buy the product—or some combination of other, unrelated factors. "Sales went up," a manager might gleefully announce, having seen the latest numbers, "so we must have gotten our money's worth." But again, not necessarily. What was the stock market doing at the time? What were competitors doing? What was Greenspan saying about future interest rates? (This matters a lot when it comes to durables with long purchase cycles.) What products were Leno and Letterman poking fun at in their opening monologues? As it happens, even the weather can have a significant impact on consumer purchase behavior. Just ask Kraft's brand manager for Country Time lemonade. Hot weather equals happy brand managers.

Before they pat themselves too firmly on the back, therefore, marketing organizations should simply realize that sales going up may actually prove little in terms of campaign effectiveness. In a systematic effort to get a more accurate read on the marketing effectiveness of their mass media efforts—and, more importantly, to improve them over time—sophisticated marketers have turned their attention in recent years to additional sources of insight. This insight has taken several forms, including a database-driven analytical approach known as *marketing mix modeling.*

As a decision support tool, marketing mix modeling enables marketers to examine the outcomes of previous campaigns, and to quantify the most effective activities for each brand and the likely sales impact for each type of media, for use in future campaigns. Interestingly, much of the information that drives marketing mix modeling is derived from the performance of national marketing plans in local markets—for example, taking the resultant exposure, as measured in GRPs, of an ad that aired during a prime-time TV series, and then comparing those GRPs to weekly sales figures in up to 50 local markets. From this data, statisticians can extrapolate that a different campaign launched under a different set of circumstances would nonetheless yield a similar set of results. Media planners can then use the analyses to guide their tactical decisions around the timing, weight, and delivery method of the new marketing messages.

To be fair, most consumer packaged goods (CPG) companies operate in a world far removed from that of many other types of companies, to the extent that they have access to enormous amounts of sales response data. Millions of natural experiments take place every year, the outcomes of which can be carefully tracked through retail loyalty card programs. As we discuss, these programs can ultimately tell marketers what would likely happen if they were to, say, change a price or run a certain type of promotion. By taking advantage of scanner panel databases, CPG companies can build large-scale models, whether they're complicated regression models, neural network approaches, or genetic algorithm optimizations. By contrast, companies without access to such databases may need to rely on other, more creative ways to capture sales response data, and precision marketing techniques may provide at least part of the solution.

Scanner panel databases feed CPG companies' marketing

mix modeling efforts, which, in turn, provide the backbone to the empirical portion of their marketing decisions, especially as they relate to resource allocation: "[Modeling] tells me what I should do more of, what I should do less of, where I should spend my money, and how much of it I should spend," notes Mike Duffy, the senior market research director at Kraft Foods.[1] He views modeling as an indispensable tool for predicting how much relative lift a certain campaign may generate, given changes in such variables as flighting, market selection, or day-part—or for gauging the relative merits of, say, marketing stand-alone versus bundled products. "Relative" is the key word; marketing mix modeling works best for helping to prioritize investments. "Most smart users of ROI measures use marketing mix modeling to rank order things," Duffy explains. This is necessary, he says, because "there are literally thousands of things a marketer can do, and only five or ten things that they're actually *going* to do."[2]

Surprisingly, these "smart users" would appear to be few and far between, as evidenced by the fact that the vendors of data analytics services, including marketing mix modeling and other forms of return-on-advertising remain part of a small cottage industry. Scott Moore, a senior vice president who heads the analytics practice at advertising giant Leo Burnett, agrees that most companies today have yet to place a premium on measuring marketing campaign effectiveness. If companies were really interested in the effects of their mass media, he observes, then firms like Hudson River Group, Marketing Management Analytics, and the portion of Nielsen Research that engages in this type of work would be a great deal larger than they are today.

He makes a good point. Today the marketing research industry remains dominated by brand awareness tracking services, Millward Brown being a notable example. These services can be valuable, helping companies to identify whether their intended marketing messages came across loud and clear. But in our view, they provide only one piece of the puzzle, as they don't begin to employ the analytical capabilities that can have a far greater impact in terms of enhancing overall marketing effectiveness.

For its part, marketing mix modeling has been shown to improve operational profits by 10 percent or more across multiple industry contexts—not just packaged goods, but also financial services and even apparel. Nonetheless, many marketing and media planners have yet to integrate the underlying data into their decision-making processes. Instead, congregating around their whiteboards, they are apt to play out various hypothetical scenarios by making gross assumptions about TV-versus-radio-versus-print-versus-online advertising responsiveness. Rarely will these assumptions be steeped in the kind of deep, scientific understanding that can be derived only from the integration and analysis of all available data across all channels and touchpoints.

Today, in fact, many planners have only a minimal understanding of the elasticity associated with their marketing allocation decisions. They will often make decisions about their advertising and trade budgets, including in-store merchandising, without really knowing what the various response curves look like. At what point does an incremental dollar spent on TV advertising become less effective than an incremental dollar spent on other types of advertising? At times, it's anybody's guess. Many marketers subscribe to syndicated sources of econometric data, including scanner panel data, from research firms like ACNielsen and Information Resources, Inc. In many cases, the information can provide meta-analyses of past marketing programs that can be used to suggest, for example, the average percentage increase in sales generated by a particular type of marketing program. Marketers can use the information, even varying the weights on certain variables, to forecast the outcomes of a new campaign under consideration.

Still, the main problem with econometric data is that it provides only a general understanding of what the outcomes might be for any given type of program, and may therefore be of limited usefulness. How applicable are the results of past campaigns in the context of future ones, anyway? Novelties wear off. People's tastes change. The mood of the entire country can change. It happens all the time. Consider a new TV series that bombs even though it followed a supposedly successful formula. (The reality TV genre offers several recent examples.) The same principle holds true for ad campaigns—although, that said, we don't dispute the need to develop general principles of what might work, based on what has worked in the past, and then verify that the same principles still apply.

The important point is that most companies, with the exception of some of the leading consumer packaged goods and financial services players, tend to apply only minimal analytical rigor to their mass marketing activities. Again, they are simply not in the habit of collecting and manipulating data in ways that can yield actionable insights. In fact, many companies may not even think of research as an integral way to do business. When marketers operate at a gut reaction level, as is often the case, the research becomes nothing more than a vague afterthought. Acting on a gut reaction is certainly cheaper than conducting extensive data analyses, but only in the short run. The better, more profitable option is to build marketing models that seek to detect exactly how much incremental volume results from each marketing dollar spent.

Marketing modeling means correlating variations on the input side with variations on the output side to discover which factors produce a desirable effect. It means filtering through the dense noise in the ocean of data that describes a particular market in an attempt to figure out how all the different marketing levers interact, and to then adjust the levers for optimal performance.

Sunil Garga, president of Marketing Management Analytics, a Wilton, Connecticut-based consultancy and the primary vendor for Kraft in the analytics area, believes that the tide is turning in terms of how companies approach marketing. He anticipates a far greater reliance on data usage to drive marketing decisions.

In fact, noting that companies can no longer afford to rely on subjective interpretations of perceived marketing outcomes, he predicts that the next couple of years will bring more change to the Marketing ROI arena than the last couple of decades combined. "The only way for a marketer to decide where to allocate spending is through a fact-based budget setting," he says, pointing to a recent surge in demand for the services his own firm offers as solid proof that more companies are finally coming to their senses.[3] No doubt, the demand for analytics-related services for mass marketing will continue to grow. In addition, the use of third-party business intelligence and technology platforms will be increasingly deployed to help companies understand their customers—and interact with them—at a narrow segmentation level, supporting the rapid expansion of their precision marketing programs. We discuss the trend toward marketing outsourcing in Chapter 4.

TREATING MARKETING AS A BUSINESS DISCIPLINE

The Chartered Institute of Marketing defines *marketing* as "the management process responsible for identifying, anticipating and satisfying customer requirements profitably." Note the use of the term *management process*. It implies that marketing is a business discipline that, like every other business discipline, ought to conform to a set of established organizational standards—which, by definition, involve measurement.

"If you can't measure it, you can't manage it," the management guru Peter Drucker is often quoted as saying. His words have long resonated with manufacturing, operations, and supply chain managers. After all, measurement permeates practically everything they do. They measure reduced error rates of orders and stock-outs. They measure the percentage of products delivered within a predetermined time range. They measure the number of products delivered within dimensional tolerances, or within an agreed-to specification, as percentages of acceptance or in parts-per-million rejections. And so on. Within the realm of marketing, however, Drucker's words have often fallen on deaf ears.

Traditionally, marketing organizations have been able to get away with spending enormous sums of money—oftentimes, a quarter or more of the company's total revenues above the cost of goods sold—without having to account for the impact on sales and profits with any degree of exactitude. For that reason, Marketing ROI has often been called "loose," "sloppy," and even "shoddy."

To be fair, Marketing ROI can be difficult to measure even for companies that have made the commitment and invested the resources. Particularly vexing is the fact that the financial systems are often not set up to track payment for marketing programs. Indeed, people who live the life of trying to tease out Marketing ROI often find that the arithmetic of the accounting can pose nearly as big a challenge as building the complicated, state-of-the-art response models. That's because, in general, the financial systems are set up to track only *total shareholder value*. The accounting and auditing activities take place at a high level, with expenditures usually tied to the market share of the brand rather than fixed amounts being earmarked for particular promotions. Furthermore, companies often make lump sum payments to their retail customers, who are authorized to spend the money as they please, across all of the different brands.

Companies can make simplifying assumptions that are adequate for tracking a company's total finances. However, the costs associated with a particular brand promotion often become hopelessly muddied up in some sound and reasonable business decisions. Again, these decisions make it easy to do business with a retail customer, but can make it next to impossible to track the actual cost of an individual promotion. Bill Bean of PepsiCo sums up the point nicely. "It's a good idea to track Marketing ROI," he says. "But it's difficult to do, not just because of the high tech, rocket science modeling, but because of the simple rules of accounting."[4]

The lack of precision around accountability and measurement has suited most employees of the marketing organization just fine. After all, few of them would *want* to assume responsibility for uncertain business outcomes if the alternative meant collecting their paychecks without having to put their necks on the line. Do marketing executives *really* want to know how well—or how poorly—their advertising dollars are paying off? ROI can upset the applecart. Again, the marketing organization can hardly be blamed for its reluctance to assume full financial responsibility, given that Marketing ROI for any given campaign or initiative has usually been nearly as hard to measure as, say, the value of a new work of art.

The art analogy is fitting. After all, some people in the industry believe marketing *is* an art, pure and simple, and wrapping it up in the cloak of measurement, statistics, and hard facts would be to suffocate the whole creative process. To them, we say: "*Hogwash.*" The creative spark of ingenuity that drives the marketing process ought to be met at every turn with fact-based decision-making. There's no other way around it, given the pressures of the marketplace and the benefits that a scientific approach can deliver in terms of increased marketing productivity. Marc Landsberg, executive vice president of corporate strategy at Publicis Groupe, echoes the sentiments of many industry practitioners when he says that "science can enable and empower the art."[5]

Scott Moore of Leo Burnett contends that most companies today still treat marketing as 80 percent to 90 percent art. Only now, he says, is marketing picking up speed as it moves in the direction of science. In his mind, the trade-offs are clear: "Treating marketing as an art, companies can achieve the big, creative ideas that are most likely to resonate with people. The problem is that the art drives the allocation decisions, so you're probably not spending the money where you want to spend it." Ideally, he says, you want to divorce the two. "It's a bit of a catch-22, because what I spend depends on the creative ideas. But I can't go out and execute a whole bunch of ideas, and then intuit the results. At the end of the day, it's going to be somewhat of an unknowable process."[6]

Marketing campaigns need to combine the science of database modeling, market segmentation, profile scoring, and predictive analytics with the art of branding and creative development. The right brain and the left brain are complementary, and need to work in tandem. Just as marketers need to leverage the synergies between mass marketing and precision marketing, and between their offline and online channels, so, too, must they marry their creative endeavors with the reality of business economics. The ability to show returns—both anticipated and real—on marketing initiatives can no longer be treated as a nice-to-have. The reason is simple. Managers, in their relentless efforts to improve the bottom line, have already squeezed the operational inefficiencies out of practically every back-office function. Even the sales process has become streamlined and automated. Most companies have simply run out of juice to squeeze. The final frontier, therefore, means attacking the biggest line item on the P&L: classic, above-the-line marketing.

Today, CEOs are mandating that every marketing dollar pay off. They are demanding that marketing be treated as one would treat any portfolio of financial investments, which is to say that at any given point in time you should know the cost of the investments as well as the anticipated returns. Again, this may mean not only graduating from a liberal arts orientation of marketing to a mathematics and science orientation, but also creating an environment wherein marketing expenditures can be closely tracked through retail customer programs. All in all, it's a rude awakening for marketing managers unaccustomed to reporting the impact of their efforts on shareholder investment.

According to a recent report by PRIMEDIA, more than 70 percent of companies are giving Marketing ROI a higher priority than ever before, with nearly 65 percent of marketers saying that top management is now involved in making marketing decisions.[7] Increasingly, the ROI for marketing will need to be in line with the ROI for every other business expenditure that managers find themselves in the position of having to rationalize, justify, and prioritize. No longer can the marketing organization claim exemption from the rules that guide every other part of the company, except perhaps for the legal counsel, the administrative staff, and the mailroom clerks. Going forward, marketers will have to show, quantitatively, that they're earning their keep— that is, if they want to avoid being reassigned to the mailroom.

INTRODUCING THE DIRECTOR
OF MARKETING ECONOMICS

Approaching marketing decision-making as less of a subjective art and more as a fact-based science, coupled with the need to create a culture of financial accountability around marketing spending, requires fundamental changes in how people think and act. For that reason, the effort to transform the marketing process into a true business discipline can't be viewed as a quick fix. Instead, it must be viewed as a philosophy that needs to be disseminated and nurtured throughout the company, to the furthest reaches of the organization (and even to partner organizations), over a period of time.

Indeed, business transformation always has a human face, with organizational adoption usually posing the biggest stumbling block to bringing a new corporate vision to fruition. Because people are generally loath to change their behavior and would ordinarily be inclined to resist the effort to treat the marketing process as a business discipline that needs to embrace analytics, measurement, and Marketing ROI, change always needs to begin at the very top of the corporate hierarchy. In the case of P&G, it was CEO A.G. Lafley who declared that the marketing organization must henceforth become accountable for its actions. For his part, Lafley has repeatedly referred to himself as "a catalyst of change" and "a coach of change management." He understands that to create organizational alignment, the context for change needs to be established by the executive leadership team.

In carrying out the change, the formula for success may simply lie in the creation of a cross-functional team that brings together strong finance people with strong marketing people, and encourages them to work together in a constructive manner. "It's more about getting the two sides to interact and engage in good communication patterns and good diplomacy than about having a structured process that has to remain the same everywhere," says Bill Mirbach, vice president of direct marketing for Intuit, the maker of Quickbooks and Quicken software.[8] When marketers are forced to drive everything they do through an ROI calculation, they start to make irrational decisions—hence the need to make the decision-making process a collaborative effort. But getting there may also mean redefining some people's roles and responsibilities.

Consider the traditional structure of the marketing planning process, and the organizational flow that surrounds it. Generally speaking, the process begins when the CFO unveils the budget. The CMO then decides how much money to allocate to each brand category across the company's portfolio of offerings. Next, the vice president of marketing decides how to divvy up the money within each of the brands. The media planning folks are awarded some of it, while another slice of the pie goes to the ad agency that determines the mass media mix. Depending on the industry, some of the money may end up in the hands of retailers who put the products on the shelves, in the form of a trade budget. Finally, some of the money may go to the director of customer relationship management—who, in turn, may divide it up between a customer acquisition and retention budget.

The structure is not highly conducive to creating a Marketing ROI mind set. Therefore, we suggest a few changes, the first of which would address the simple fact that, in many companies, the CMO is not a P&L person. This fact helps explain why tensions often erupt between the CEO and the CFO (incidentally, our first suggestion is that the CMO report directly to the CEO, to avert the conflicts of interest that invariably arise between the manufacturing operations of a company and the economic results of its marketing decisions). It may also help explain why, in many industries, the CMO has an average tenure of only 18 months.

With each budget cycle, the CFO invests x amount of money into the marketing organization, often with little to show for it in the way of tangible returns other than a handful of press mentions and brand awareness studies. The marketing organization may track internal goals, such as the number of leads it generates and the cost per lead, but it seldom quantifies the outcomes of its marketing efforts in ways that tie deliverables to customer acquisition, retention, or leverage metrics, or any other increases in shareholder value. Rather, it typically falls on the sales organization to report the sales numbers and quantify the returns on investment—and to also take the credit when sales meet or exceed revenue goals.

With the rise of precision marketing, the marketing organization can now get its due. Suddenly it has at its disposal a whole new set of metrics to report and track against—metrics that can be directly linked to top-line revenue growth. Precision marketing is results oriented. Unlike the outcomes of mass marketing programs, which often seem shrouded in vague promises of incremental lift, the outcomes of precision marketing programs are almost always knowable, and usually within a matter of days or weeks rather than months or quarters. That being the case, precision marketing can empower the CMO by equipping him with ammunition to better meet the CEO's demands for increased financial responsibility. Again, the CMO has traditionally had no line responsibility whatsoever, and has instead tended to focus his attention on the execution of tactics such as sales support, public relations, and marketing campaigns, as well as the overall strategic direction of the brands. With increased financial responsibility at least comes the availability of a new set of tools for managing and measuring Marketing ROI.

Having adopted a Marketing ROI mind set, the CMO might be

advised to take out a boundary-spanning marker and draw a thick line down the middle of the organization. On one side would be those people who set the marketing objectives, and on the other side would be those people who execute the programs. A good organizational model might be to simply say, "Okay, finance guys, you tell the marketers what their allowable cost per order is, and you figure it out depending on the business needs, as defined by the senior manager." It's foolish to make marketing managers sit around and grind numbers when their time could be better spent identifying unmet customer needs, or dreaming up new marketing campaigns, or even arm wrestling with vendors for cheaper ad space. "I want the marketers to market and the finance guys to set the limits," says Bill Mirbach of Intuit. "That works a lot better for us."[9]

So, the best way to resolve the internal conflict that exists within many companies with respect to Marketing ROI may be to simply divorce the Art from the Science. Create two separate functions, in essence, and let each one do what it does best. Let Art focus on messages, ideas, and creative management, and let Science focus on the analytics of data management, as well as the underlying economics of the overall marketing program. To that end, we propose that companies create a new executive position: *the director of marketing economics.* Reporting directly to the CMO, the person holding this position would oversee all activities related to Marketing ROI. The job description would likely vary, depending on the specifics of the company's portfolio and purview. In all cases, however, the resource allocation questions would naturally flow from a customer-centric perspective. For example: "Which customer segments should we spend money on, and what are the products and brands that flow from those segments?" "How much should we spend on customer acquisition versus retention, and what should the corresponding programs look like?" "How much should we spend on mass marketing programs, and what are the different vehicles within mass marketing to which we would want to allocate funds?" "How much should we spend on precision marketing programs, and what are the different vehicles within precision marketing to which we would want to allocate funds?" And so on.

Decoupling the economic issues from the creative process would allow marketers to focus on how to maximize dollars with ideas. Right now, the economics and the ideas are mutually dependent. Companies need to free them from one another, and the appointment of a director of marketing economics may be the best way to create that force of liberation.

Interestingly, the structure of the marketing organization would then come to bear a striking resemblance to the classic Hollywood studio model. The role of the director of marketing economics would be akin to that of the executive producer on the studio lot, responsible for setting the budget and determining the time frame within which the project needs to be completed. While the executive producer has the ultimate responsibility for the project's successful completion, the creative decisions are usually left to the director. In the marketing organization, the director's counterpart would be the brand or marketing manager who oversees the agency's creative development efforts.

THE PRECISION MARKETING CYCLE

The pressure to shore up the economic side of the marketing equation is helping to expedite the advancement of customer analytics and robust segmentation, as we've already suggested, converting a soft science into a hard science, and ultimately ushering in a new marketing mind set. Indeed, the methodologies that underlie precision marketing can be every bit as rigorous—in other words, as *statistically valid*—as those that Deming came to apply in the context of industrial operations management. (Given the scope of this book, we do not discuss multivariate, nonlinear, stochastic differential equations, except to say that such equations are the intellectual core of many of the advances that have been made in modern society—and are now being applied to the realm of marketing, with impressive results.)

The Precision Marketing Cycle serves as the conceptual foundation for the overall precision marketing process. It consists of four basic stages, as shown in Figure 2.1. The stages are described in some detail in the following sections, along with examples of precision marketing programs that we or others have recently implemented.

Stage 1: Determine the Objective and Collect the Data Profiles

As *Alice in Wonderland*'s Cheshire Cat so deftly observed, if you don't know where you're going, any road will take you there. The Precision Marketing Cycle starts with a need to define the specific objectives for the marketing program. What does the program aim to accomplish in terms of tangible business benefits?

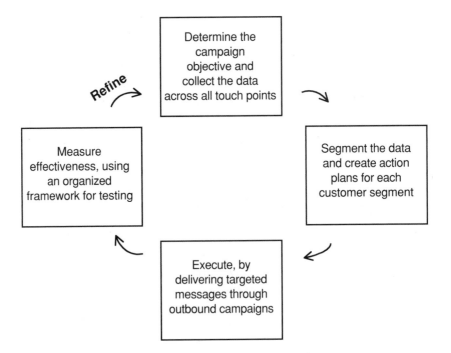

FIGURE 2.1   The Precision Marketing Cycle

Again, these benefits might take any number of forms, provided each of them eventually translates into increased revenues and profitability. Envisaging how a precision marketing program will advance the company's overall efforts to do what marketing is supposed to do—get more people to buy your product or service—is the first stop along the journey.

Campaign budgets and time lines should always be driven by the business objectives. So, too, should the various tactical aspects of the campaign, including target market selection, channel selection, incentives selection, campaign duration, and measurement unit selection, as well as the key parameters around the target cost per customer, the number of data fields to be completed per customer, if appropriate, and the target response rate. Creative development should then flow naturally from the configuration of these tactical aspects.

The business objectives should be articulated in terms that can be easily quantified and subsequently measured—for example, "to capture such and such information about new customer prospects," or "to expand such and such information about customer segment Y," or "to generate x amount of incremental revenue by cross-selling such and such offerings to customer segment Y." Again, a stated objective that falls along the lines of "to raise overall brand awareness" may have garnered significant support in the past, and may be ample reason for many companies to continue to spend large sums of money on mass marketing campaigns à la Madison Avenue. But such a vague, open-ended objective has no place in the world of precision marketing, where mathematical models and rules-based decision support systems run the show.

Capturing relevant data is the sine qua non of precision marketing. As it happens, customer relationship repositories are often data rich and information poor, just as customer bases are often expansive in terms of the *number* of customers but shallow in terms of the *profitability* of most of those customers. This phenomenon of information-poor repositories helps explain why some companies can spend lavishly to build data-mining capabilities, but can still fail to achieve significant cost reduction outcomes or improved cross-sales performance. A company may learn more than it ever thought possible about customer behavior and characteristics, but ultimately fail to convert this newfound knowledge into dollars, yen, or euros—in effect, defeating the purpose of the initiative.

Knowing the business objective on the front end informs exactly what types of information a precision marketing program should seek to obtain. Therefore, a key question to ask in the course of planning such a program should be: "What personal information do we already have about our customers, and what additional information do we need to collect in order to round out their profiles in a meaningful way?" More to the point: "What missing data fields do we want registrants to fill in?" Does program success hinge on knowing their food allergies? Their professional aspirations? Their favorite rock bands? Whether they practice yoga? Whether they buy presents for their dogs? What kind of cars they drive? After that, it becomes a matter of backing up into an effective strategy for persuading people to provide the missing pieces of information.

The Internet provides a perfect environment for conducting response-based surveys, which can be used to decode customer interests, preferences, and personalities. Take a simple example: On vacation, would you prefer to be in . . . the great outdoors, an art museum, or your own kitchen? On the weekend, would you prefer to . . . trek up a mountain peak, conquer the nearest outlet mall, or make a chocolate soufflé? Stranded on a deserted island, would you prefer to have . . . a guitar, a mirror, or a cast-iron skillet? File respondents who select option number three across the board into the customer segment labeled Quintessential Gourmets. Members of this club may be excellent candidates to receive marketing offers for pasta machines, cake decorating books, and any kitchen utensil that measures, chops, or slices.

Sophisticated survey designs may deplore *discreet choice analysis.* Marketers can use this methodology to simulate all potential offers, and determine which levers a customer would more likely respond to. For example: How important is it for you to have . . . the best price? A good return policy? A knowledgeable sales rep to explain the different product features and functionalities? A marketer may offer choices at multiple iterations, using response-based surveys to ask the same questions in different fashions so as to begin to isolate the various levers that are at the forefront of the purchase decision.

In many cases, therefore, the initial rounds of a precision marketing program may be solely devoted to capturing the information that enables the company to create a description of a customer's stated preferences, in advance of any actual selling activity. These initial rounds lay the necessary groundwork for a successful campaign. Fact is, you can't go out and buy a mailing list from the motor vehicle registry, the post office, or any other third-party source that contains the names and addresses of people who earn more than $75K and also like to arrive at airports at least two hours early. Or parents with young children who dine out at least twice a week. Or men who snack on low-fat ice cream while watching late-night TV. Knowing these seemingly trivial and arbitrary pieces of information may, in fact, be absolutely crucial, and collecting the information directly and voluntarily, as opposed to buying it (even if it were available) from third parties, is key to honoring the integrity of the *consensual customer*, as we discuss in Chapter 5.

In general, building a robust customer profile that provides a bounty of marketing insights means pulling together numerous databases and inputs, both internal and external. It requires the use of *explicit data* (information collected through direct customer response and entry), *implicit data* (information collected through direct observation of customer activity), and *derived data* (new insights developed through data analysis and modeling). Offline-to-online campaigns—also described as mass-marketing-to-precision-marketing programs—can be key to facilitating the acquisition of explicit data, provided that the mechanism for value exchange is sufficiently compelling from the customer standpoint to warrant participation. In most cases, this includes agreeing to be the ongoing target of future promotional messages.

Having settled on what personal information needs to be collected to ensure success, and how it will be used over time to further the business objectives, it becomes important to put a price tag on that information. By doing so, the marketing organization will be in a better position to determine what rewards to offer in exchange for people's willingness to participate. The cost of the rewards also needs to be factored into the Marketing ROI equation.

Of course, carrots come in many different flavors. The incentives commonly used to drive people to a website registration page and to get them to complete the process may include discounts, bonus points, and product samples. Nonmonetary incentives, including information updates and access to exclusive content, can also get people to bite. Contests and sweepstakes, in particular, can provide effective enticements for capturing personal information from both new and existing customers, and also for securing their permission to engage in future marketing activities. One online contest generated more than a half million e-mail addresses by offering a prize of free gas for a year.

In 2003, Pepsi's wildly hyped Play for a Billion sweepstakes allowed the company to meet its mass marketing objectives around brand awareness. The promotion also allowed the company's loyalty management group to capture the names, e-mails, ages, and mailing addresses of new Pepsi drinkers, along with permission to shower them with biweekly updates about promotions, events, and products—no matter that there was only a one in one thousand chance that the grand prize would even be awarded.

It was back in 2000 that Pepsi launched its first offline-to-online program, called Pepsi Stuff, allowing consumers to earn digital awards from promotional partners. The database consisted of two million names. The Play for a Billion promotion more than doubled the size of that database. No doubt, its 2004

Pepsi iTunes promotion will have doubled it once again. Marketing executives at Pepsi are convinced that regular e-mail communication with these sweepstakes entrants increases their Pepsi consumption. "We have evidence that our targeted marketing works really well for us," noted Bill Bean. "We can drive volume increases in that group with fairly cheap, minimal contact by nice, healthy increments."[10] As Pepsi's buyer base goes, a few million names is fairly insignificant. Still, it's large enough to provide proof-of-concept that precision marketing can be an important piece of the marketing mix, and one that will become increasingly important going forward.

Pepsi is hardly alone in the effort to drive consumers to online response forms. These days, one doesn't have to look far at all to find countless examples of traditional mass media marketers using offline-to-online programs to capture customer information, from TV ads for Pizza Hut ("Get great online deals when you register at PizzaHut.com.") to radio announcements for McDonald's ("What is an NBA Platinum Pass? It's the ultimate hoops hook-up from Mickey D's. Enter today and show off your VIP handles."). United Airlines invites readers of *People* magazine to "instantly win a trip to play Chris Evert and sit courtside at the 2003 U.S. Open finals." But, of course, you gotta play to win.

Direct mail can be another catalyst to get people to fill in the blanks. Consider a precision marketing program that we developed for DeWalt Industrial Tool Company, a leading manufacturer of power tools and accessories. Here the business objective was to capture the e-mail addresses of existing customers whose profile records, compiled based on information gleaned over the years from returned manufacturers' warranty cards, were incomplete and/or outdated. We settled on a direct-mail campaign using PopOut Window Postcards from WebDecoder, a product of Global Commerce Group. The postcards invite recipients to go to a page on the DeWalt website. Holding the viewing window of the postcard up to a blue spot that appears on the screen reveals a prize code. To find out if the code is a winner, however, you first have to enter the updated contact information—a minor inconvenience, given a chance to win a new circular saw.

Compared to manufacturers of power tools, many grocery store retailers have a distinct advantage when it comes to collecting customer data. After all, they can already know, at an individual household level, who buys their products—thanks largely to the services offered by market research and shopper data firms like Catalina Marketing Corporation and Knowledge Networks/Promotion Decisions. These firms also serve as a conduit that enables many of the nation's largest CPG companies to communicate with their end-customers, based on those customers' specific purchase behavior. In the world of CPG-based precision marketing, these vendors can provide much of the essential plumbing.

For example, CPG companies can use correlation analysis to target customers who already buy products in certain categories with offers to buy other products in tangential categories. Assume you buy cashew butter. Maybe a manufacturer wants to send all cashew butter aficionados an incentive to sample its new brand of almond butter, given the likelihood that people who enjoy one variety of nut butter may also enjoy other varieties. Almond butter may be a 10-percent penetration category. As such, it's a foregone conclusion that if, say, a 25-cents-off coupon were printed and distributed in a freestanding insert, at least 90 percent of recipients would disregard it. The story would play out very differently, however, if a cashier were to physically place a 25-cents-off in-store coupon in the hands of only those shoppers who already buy cashew butter—which is exactly what firms like Catalina and KN/PDI give CPG companies the power to do.

Or consider a competitive promotion, in which case a shopper might buy a two-liter bottle of Vanilla Coke. The UPC for that bottle is scanned in a supermarket, and instantly that person receives a coupon for a two-liter bottle of Vanilla Pepsi. For its part, Pepsi doesn't know who that person is, where he or she lives, or what his or her personal attitude might be toward a particular product. All Pepsi knows is that a shopper walked into a store and bought its competitor's product, and that Pepsi then offered that same shopper an incentive to change behavior the next time he or she walks into a store.

Note, also, that in-store coupons can serve as yet another catalyst that can enable a CPG company to capture end-customers' e-mail addresses and gain permission to directly market to them. Consider a recent campaign by P&G in which shoppers who bought Cascade dishwashing detergent automatically received an invitation to visit Cascade's website for a chance to enter a monthly sweepstakes drawing. Playing meant not only providing contact information, but also answering a series of questions about their family's dishwashing habits—again, a small price to pay for a shot at winning a year's supply of Power Tabs rinse aids.

Website response forms represent only one of several ways to capture customer information. In 2003, starting with its Olay Daily Facial product, P&G began experimenting with automated inbound teleservices and speech-to-text technology. The print advertisement for the product featured a 1-900-TRY-OLAY hotline that people could call to request a product sample. A recorded voice at the Daily Facial Sample Request Line asked callers a series of questions, including age and e-mail address, to which they were to verbally respond. As the technology improves, offline-to-phone campaigns will play a larger role in helping marketers to obtain information about new customers while deepening the profile information of existing customers.

Finally, consider warranty cards and rebate forms as vehicles for getting customers to pony up information, including their future purchase intentions. For example, consumers who buy a new dishwasher from KitchenAid are asked to complete a product registration form, ostensibly for the purpose of speeding up service in the event of a product recall, and also to verify ownership in the event of product loss or theft. But these explanations hardly account for the string of questions that are asked above and beyond basic contact information. For example:

Tell us about your appliances.

Refrigerator	Brand _____	Approximate Age _____
Range/Cooktop	Brand _____	Approximate Age _____
Microwave	Brand _____	Approximate Age _____
Washer	Brand _____	Approximate Age _____
Dryer	Brand _____	Approximate Age _____

Customers are asked to indicate which appliances they plan to replace within the next year, and to also provide a host of other information, including occupation and income. Will knowing this information help KitchenAid service you in the event of a product recall? Not likely. But it will certainly help KitchenAid sell you more stuff.

Stage 2: Segment Data Profiles and Create Action Plans

Recently, for no apparent reason, editors at the *New York Times* decided to look at patterns of dog ownership by Zip code in New York City. What they found, based on their analysis of dog licensing data, was reinforcement of some longstanding stereotypes. For example, the Shih Tzu breed was most predominant in the Upper East Side. The Chihuahua, which rose to fame thanks to its starring role in Taco Bell ads, was most popular in Spanish Harlem. The intimidating Rottweiler lives mostly in the South Bronx. And so on. Segmenting dogs by breed provided some front-page amusement for early-morning commuters.

Segmenting people according to common traits, needs, or interest areas is more serious business, because it allows companies to talk to them about the benefits of their products or services in a specific way. The next step in the Precision Marketing Cycle, therefore, is to cluster each set of customers into discrete groups based on their behaviors, usage patterns, and any other criteria that may make sense in the context of the overall business objectives. This should be done with a line of sight to then developing individual action plans for each customer segment.

Segmentation schemes, while not always readily apparent, eventually bubble to the surface. "I've never seen a data set that could not be segmented," boasted one research analyst. In fact, segmentation studies are usually easy to do, but difficult to harness. In general, the key is to incorporate an economic component—that is, determine the exact amount of value that each segment generates—and to then "talk" to each segment in a context-sensitive way, using precision marketing techniques. Often, the biggest challenge comes in trying to translate the segmentation scheme into a language that makes practical sense from a marketer's perspective. "You can always find customers that by many measures are more profitable to you than other customers," noted one marketer. "You just need to take into account how much it costs you to get them."

Creating effective segmentation schemes may depend more on response-based segmentation than on the traditional sociodemographic classifications we outline in the previous chapter. Typically, these latter classifications involve looking at basic household-level data such as current income, educational attainment, and presence of children. The data, available from any number of vendors, comes in myriad forms and formats, as well as varying degrees of accuracy and comprehensiveness, and can be sliced and diced in multiple ways. The data can provide a solid foundation for just about any segmentation scheme; taken by itself, however, it invariably paints only a fuzzy and incomplete picture of customers.

In 2001, Comcast Communications, the largest U.S. cable company, used sociodemographic data to launch a direct mail campaign designed to acquire new subscribers to its digital cable offering. Comcast divided the target audience into seven core groups: Affluent Family, Suburban Family, Ethnic Urban, Blue Collar, Hispanic, Baby Boomers, and Young & Mobile. For its efforts, Comcast was awarded a coveted Mark Award from the Cable & Telecommunications Association for Marketing, which noted that the company had never before taken such a "highly targeted approach" to speaking to "each target audience's unique lifestyle and interests."[11] But while the lavish praise heaped on Comcast suggests that the company was taking precision marketing to a new level, the segmentation scheme shows no such sign of innovation, leaving us to wonder: Why the fuss?

Response-based segmentation leverages proprietary, primary-sourced data captured through precision marketing techniques. The data is context specific. It fills in the white spaces left by sociodemographic segmentation to paint a far more vivid and complete picture of customers. Often, the data reflects customers' stated preferences, intentions, and mind sets. It can reveal different emotions, moods, and psyches that, in turn, should trigger different marketing treatments. Does the customer . . . Place more value on time or money? Require a lot of technical support? Seem eager to indulge himself? Place a premium on durability? Consider herself to be practical minded? Want to lose weight and get into shape? Feel emotional about a particular brand? Need to get organized? Want to express uniqueness and individuality? Feel like trying something new? Favor small, blue devices? People relate to these types of questions along different dimensions, and they place varying amounts of importance on each dimension. By grouping together customers with similar response patterns—and again, by understanding their economic value—companies can often market to them in highly effective ways.

For example, a credit card company may wish to create a campaign that speaks to the mind set of someone who's young and affluent, and—furthermore—who doesn't mind incurring personal debt. The company can aggregate customers whose *yes* or *no* answers to certain questions posed on the response forms would indicate that they subscribe to this particular mind set. The company can then develop an effective messaging program around the mind set, and direct it to only those customers who fit the bill. Targeting a population of young people whose stated preferences indicate that they would enjoy the benefit of a large credit line with a high APR over that of a small credit line with a low APR is a far cry from carpet bombing the millions of people who happen to be, say, Young & Mobile.

Response-based segmentation uses a post hoc approach that relies on collected data to derive the market segments, as opposed to the traditional a priori approach, which starts with preconceived notions about segment profiles, in the hope of then discovering benefit differences. Incidentally, it's important to dispel any preconceived notions about the topography of the different market segments and to simply allow the data to speak for itself. In the process, the data may generate some "ahas!s" that would otherwise have gone unnoticed.

As we've suggested, most companies are likely to have both types of segmentation frameworks in place, and to use them in conjunction with one another. The frameworks should support a company's need to look at the *total opportunity* with respect to a customer relationship. This usually means looking at the customer relationship in a different way from in the past, and looking at the opportunity to serve the broader range of a customer's needs. Extensive segmentation on an ongoing basis serves to increase customer knowledge as companies add more and more layers of detail to their pictures of customers. Traditionally, mass marketers have approached segmentation with a well-defined, ongoing hypothesis, usually along the following lines:

1. Apply a needs-based segmentation scheme.

2. Determine which market segment to target, based on whichever one ranks the highest in terms of perceived revenue potential.

3. Look at demographic and psychographic characteristics of the segment to slightly improve the mass media targeting effort.

Marketing resources would then be used to create brand positioning strategies designed to resonate with the one segment that would appear to account for the bulk of the core customer base and present the greatest growth potential. Rarely have companies devoted much attention to the runners-up, given the prohibitive costs associated with using mass media vehicles to pursue on-the-fence peripheral consumers. (Someday, perhaps, marketers will recount these constraints with a sense of nostalgia and bemusement, in much the same way that grandparents recount the days before the arrival of television: "That's right, our target market was Housewives, and that's where we placed our bets." In a world where precision marketing is the norm, it will sound like child's play.)

No doubt, companies will continue to allocate most of their marketing resources to targeting the prime prospects—which, again, will be defined at a granular, multifaceted level. And they will continue to hold planning sessions with media buyers on segments that are most profitable, de-emphasizing segments that are least profitable and ensuring that the media mix skews accordingly. At the same time, companies will then also target as many other segments as they deem desirable, including those that may be only marginally profitable. We're already seeing this trend, with some companies using mass media to target one primary segment, and then using precision marketing to target several microsegments resident within the mass market. Of course, these companies may not yet think of the process as a formal construct.

Ideally, segmentation should be approached as a set of strategic choices. In reality, there may be a thousand different ways to segment any given market. It's important to carefully weigh the pros and cons of each option. In the end, it may make sense to mix and blend the different options. There are no hard and fast rules, since the segments can always be redefined with a simple flick of the switch, given the flexibility of data cell architecture. Nothing is written in stone. Also, bear in mind that, for practically any categorization scheme, some consumers are bound to straddle multiple segments.

For every customer relationship, a company may eventually collect a hundred different data points, many of which may seem to be highly relevant in terms of defining the different segments. The question is, What combination of these data points would *really* cause a segment to be identified in a unique and meaningful way from a marketing perspective? Identifying unique segments of sufficient scale by which to organize the customer base is rarely an easy task. To keep things simple, many companies have adopted a "less is more" approach, creating segmentation schemes comprised of no more than half a dozen or so high-level categories as a starting point.

Consider SBC Communications, which ranks as one of the world's leading data, voice, and Internet service providers. In 2002, SBC took a hard look at its customer database and arrived at the following segmentation scheme:

~ Tech-centrics (mostly young people comfortable with technology features and functionality).

~ Golden Years (older people who may be less technology savvy).

~ Moving on Up (college educated, upwardly mobile professionals).

~ SUVs and Soccer Balls (suburban families with school-age children).

~ Getting By (working people with limited discretionary spending).

~ Old Faithful (long-time, loyal customers).

Having segmented the market in this way, how might a company like SBC then formulate and deliver a marketing message geared to a particular category? By making—and later verifying, through both in-market and out-of-market testing—a series of assumptions about the needs and characteristics of that segment. Take the Tech-centrics, for example. It's probably safe to assume that the members of this club would desire services like wireless and broadband DSL, as well as any newly released features now available for their handhelds. Also, it would probably make sense to create an attractive package that ties all of these different offerings together. And, furthermore, because Tech-centrics are likely to have a high comfort level interacting and transacting online, it only stands to reason that SBC would reach out to them using the Internet as their preferred channel of communication.

Or consider a segmentation scheme in the $1.5 billion skin care products category. People have a variety of different skin care needs, depending on their medical condition, their age, their ethnicity, the geography and climate in which they live, and so on. Unilever, which markets several leading skin care product lines, including Lux, Pond's, and Dove, chose to segment the skin care market into six high-level categories, as follows:

1. Apathetic Annie (women who spend minimal time caring for their skin).

2. Age Defying Beauty Queens (older women concerned with wrinkles, sagging, and puffy eyes).

3. Young Beauty Queens (girls with oily skin, mostly concerned with pimples and blackheads).

4. Peaches & Cream (women who want to achieve a healthy, clean, natural look; want nongreasy and hypoallergenic ingredients).

5. Dazed & Confused (women who view face care as complicated; their goal is radiant, younger-looking skin).

6. Jaded Jane (women who are skeptical of product efficacy).

According to Randy Quinn, senior vice president of brand development, Unilever can identify consumers who have skin that's prone to a particular issue through response surveys and modeling—and then, through appropriate segmentation, can market to them "with a very specific message about the benefits of a particularly formulated product via the Internet, e-mail, or a direct mail newsletter."[12] People within each of the different market segments receive the corresponding version of the newsletter, delivered through the channel of their choice.

Stage 3: Execute

The execute stage of the Precision Marketing Cycle involves the use of customer data to create customized, context-sensitive offers. Assume, for example, that Cingular wants to promote text messaging as an add-on feature. The company can use precision marketing to pare its 23 million customers down to the 1 million customers who have the greatest propensity to subscribe to that service. The cost difference between sending out 23 million direct mail pieces with a very low return and 1 million direct mail pieces with a very high return can run into the millions of dollars, considering that direct marketing communications can cost anywhere from 35 to 95 cents per piece. "With each promotion," says Mike Dobbs, vice president of product marketing, "we're mapping whatever the product happens to be to the most appropriate segment, based on everything we know about their usage habits, to get the most bang for buck." He adds that the strategy is also a win for customers tired of being inundated with irrelevant offers: "We only send offers that we know they're going to find meaningful and valuable."[13]

The execute stage assumes that a sufficient amount of relevant information about each customer has already been collected—and that, in the case of e-mail communications, customers have opted in to receive marketing messages. Consider an example from RBC Royal Bank, which ranks as Canada's largest financial services institution. Recently, the bank launched a precision marketing campaign around its Registered Education Savings Plans (RESPs). The program began by identifying more than 100,000 existing customers with young children—call it the Existing Customers with Children Who Don't Already Have an RESP Club. The bank sent the members of this club a direct mail piece containing a newsletter and a survey. The newsletter was designed to educate them about RESPs, and to encourage them to open one. For returning the completed survey, recipients were offered a chance to win $4,000 toward their child's RESP. The program reportedly exceeded the response rate goal, with five percent of recipients contributing to their child's RESP within a three-month period. Meanwhile, the survey furnished the bank with important information about its RESP customers.

One company to spotlight on the precision marketing stage is Tesco. The number one grocery retailer in the United Kingdom, Tesco may also be the number one precision marketing company on the planet, thanks to its Clubcard Program, which is used to attract, retain, and leverage 13 million customer relationships. With help from dunnhumby, a U.K.-based consultancy, Tesco has done a phenomenal job of understanding customer transaction and loyalty patterns. It knows what people buy and what they don't buy, and it understands price sensitivity, such that promotions are used not to subsidize but to drive incremental purchases. In a highly competitive industry where margins are low and nontraditional competitors are constantly stealing market share, Tesco has reported incredible results in terms of market share growth and profitability. In fact, since the program's launch in 1995, revenue has grown 51 percent (while floor space has grown only 15 percent).

Tesco understands what each type of customer values most in terms of lifestyle preferences, and it then uses this knowledge to create value for all stakeholders. How? By offering a rewards program that invites customers to join one or more clubs, whether it's a Baby Club for "mums-to-be," a World of Wine Club for wine connoisseurs or a Me Time Club, aimed at women hoping to qualify for "free pampering sessions." By tracking more than 200 million in-store purchases every day across all stores, the company has developed some 5,000 customer "needs" segments. Based on these segments, it sends out some *300,000 variations* of any given offer (redemption rates are 90 percent!) to its 10 million household customers, and upwards of *2 million permutations* for every quarterly Clubcard statement mailing. It's this level of microsegment customization that makes Tesco the most sophisticated customer communications program in Europe, and possibly the world.

The Clubcard Program saves Tesco more than £300 million a

year—again, thanks to customer data analytics that allow it to offer discounts only to price-sensitive customers, and only on products they buy. Indeed, much of Tesco's success can be attributed to promotion effectiveness; the retailer constantly evaluates the impact of its marketing campaigns against tightly defined target audiences and selects promotions that focus on rewarding *loyal customers*, as opposed to *promiscuous consumers*. The amount of data that Tesco collects and the degree to which it analyzes the data to guide its promotional offers with targeted messages may seem staggering. In truth, Tesco has merely succeeded in doing what every marketer should strive to do—that is, develop relationships with customers that make it worth their while to disclose information about themselves, and then to analyze and leverage the data to everyone's mutual benefit.

Kraft Foods offers another good example. In 2002, the company launched a print magazine, called *Food & Family*, to complement its popular Kraft Kitchen website. Published quarterly, the magazine is delivered to the homes of 2.1 million Kraft customers across the country, making it the largest circulation magazine of its kind in the United States (Tesco's *Clubcard* magazine reaches an astounding 7.5 million customers in Europe). In terms of content, the magazine offers "family meal solutions" with—surprise, surprise—Kraft products as integral components of those solutions. "We target the magazine only to those folks who we think are going to make a difference," notes Mike Duffy.[14]

In particular, Kraft identifies households that are buying Kraft products and sends them the magazine. Using scanner data, Kraft can gather store sales information in various readers' areas and gain a fairly accurate read on sales impact just nine days after issue distribution. "We know who reads it, we have a general sense of where they live, and we know roughly where they shop," says Duffy. "We don't have to wait for data to accumulate. Instead, we've created a very powerful means for providing ROI measurement on a nearly real-time basis."[15]

Kraft got immediate payback from *Food & Family* in the form of a clear and sustainable lift in sales revenues. What's perhaps most interesting in the context of the current discussion is the fact that the magazine comes in no fewer than 32 flavors, each one tailored to a primary customer segment. A consumer magazine that has 32 customized versions, and that enables marketers to track the resultant sales lift, speaks volumes about the power of precision marketing.

Stage 4: Measure Effectiveness

The need to measure marketing effectiveness, using an organized framework for testing, constitutes the final stage of the Precision Marketing Cycle. Mass media advertising produces "brand awareness," which is often measurable only in subjective terms, as we've said. Converting the softer outcomes into a financial measure is often fraught with difficulty. The payback from loyalty programs can be particularly difficult to measure in the short term.

Precision marketing, on the other hand, operates under the auspices of the scientific method, producing financial results that usually *can* be measured in the short term. Precision marketing programs can be tested against a control group to determine the specific impact on the underlying business objectives. In most cases, the test group and control group are both well-defined and clearly identifiable. The key to measurement success, then, is to compare the lift differential, as demonstrated by the test group, relative to what the brand would have otherwise achieved, as demonstrated by the control group.

In measuring financial results, companies should look at either dollar revenue or some equivalent unit measure. Kraft Foods, for one, would never use product units as its sales measure—for example, how many boxes of Jell-o did the company sell last week. "That's a silly number," says one company insider. "The only person interested in that number is our packaging department, to know how much cardboard to order. Some boxes are big, some are small. Some are four-serve, some are six-serve. Some are expensive flavors, some are cheap flavors. Some are gelatin, some are pudding. Boxes don't tell us what the sales really were." Sales data is an especially poor indicator when marketers have to work with a nested set of equations; predicting marketing effectiveness for prescription drugs, for example, requires that marketers first predict doctor acceptance and their propensity to prescribe the drugs.

Tracking and measuring marketing effectiveness has always posed a big challenge within the pharmaceutical industry. While marketing managers get detailed sales data on physician-prescribing behavior, it's usually difficult for them to understand what factors are motivating the sale. To address the larger problem of sales rep access to physicians, some pharmaceutical firms are beginning to use "eDetailing" to reach doctors. With some 96 percent of physicians now online, marketing managers are finding that a 10-minute online product presentation is a convenient way to reach those hard-to-see doctors. And since physicians must log in to the secure eDetail site, it's easy to compare exposure to an eDetail with a lift in sales data as compared to a control group to determine Marketing ROI. There is an even greater benefit than just tracking the ROI of this channel, however, according to David Ormesher, CEO of closerlook and one of the leading providers of relationship marketing solutions to the pharmaceutical industry. "What our clients are finding is that this online relationship with their customers gives them tremendous insight into individual attitudes and interests. Now we can fine-tune the customer segmentation and directly measure the ROI impact of different marketing messages on both attitudes and behavior. This gives the brand team valuable insight into where to invest and where to divest."[16]

Because every interaction with a customer enriches the company's information base, the next step is to use analytic capabilities to refine the process for the next go-round, thereby continuously improving marketing effectiveness. These analytic capabilities are varied, as we've suggested, depending on program sophistication, business objectives, and industry context. Customer transaction data, registration profile data, promotion redemption data, channel preference data, life cycle value data, product affinity data, and even buying motivation data can all feed the segmentation, campaign management, and predictive models that drive a precision marketing program.

The important point is that a precision marketing program is not a one-shot deal. Instead, it's a *recursive process*, to use a mathematical term. Multiple stages may be required to capture and interpret all of the requisite data, and also to communicate all of the desired marketing messages that, if all goes well, will ultimately culminate in one or more transactions. The front-end effort may require that customers complete a series of profile surveys over an extended period of time, with appropriate incentives in place for each subsequent round, while the company also attempts to draw additional inferences by incorporating transactional time-series data—for example, flights on an airline, calls on a cell phone, or charges to a credit card. The back-end effort may require that companies use multiple tactics, channels, and segmentation schemes in their cross-sell and up-sell efforts, also over an extended period of time. In the end, success rides on being able to capture, analyze, and act on customer data in meaningful ways, to foster a corporate mind set for experimentation and campaign testing, and to create strategic relationships with customer-facing partners.

THERE'S SOMETHING SPECIAL ABOUT CATALINA

One company that stands out from the crowd as an enabler of precision marketing programs is Catalina Marketing Corporation. That's because, in handling approximately 250 million transactions per week across more than 21,000 grocery stores, the company can provide consumer packaged goods (CPG) companies with exact information about *which* individual customers bought their products— *when, where,* and *how often.* In effect, Catalina bridges the gap between buyers and sellers, transcending a reseller channel that would ordinarily make the customer data all but out of reach.

"We can provide a tremendous amount of insight into consumption by way of our database," notes CMO Rick Mansfield. "We can then link that insight directly with access to our consumers." It may be true. The company may indeed provide the best consumer insight capabilities of any firm in the grocery industry, thanks to its unique, patent-protected ability to capture and store transaction-level data.

It may also be true, as some critics assert, that Catalina is the most costly way to reach those consumers. "It's unlikely that we would ever use Catalina as the cornerstone of our promotional program," notes one marketing executive. "It's too expensive." In fact, according to these critics, a Catalina program can cost many times more than a typical direct mail program. Catalina has also been accused of having a particular prejudice, one that has irked some manufacturers. "Their assumption is that once a consumer has used a promotion from Catalina, they're 100 percent converted to the promotional product for life," notes another observer. "It's not necessarily true, yet it's built into the company's lifetime value equations for charging the amount of money that they do."

Is Catalina worth the money? Many CPG companies certainly seem to think so.

At its core, Catalina is in the business of collecting frequent shopper data, as are parts of ACNielsen, IRI, and several other large vendors. What distinguishes Catalina from the other research firms is, first of all, the size of its household panel. ACNielsen and IRI both rely on household panels that use remote-control scanners to record UPCs of the products they buy when they return home from the grocery store. At best, these panels may number 60,000 households (although ACNielsen plans to double the size of its pool by 2005). "Our household panel is 100 million households," boasts Mansfield.*

The "Does size matter?" debate aside ("There are very few instances where the entire universe of consumer data is required," argue the critics), the fact of the matter is that, to some extent, comparing Catalina to ACNielsen and IRI is like comparing apples to oranges. ACNielsen and IRI are in business to sell frequent shopper data to manufacturers for research purposes. Catalina, on the other hand, is in business to sell promotions to manufacturers, and the

---

*Interview with Rick Mansfield by Jeff Zabin, July 11, 2003.

firm makes its money not by selling data (in fact, Catalina doesn't provide manufacturers with raw data) but by executing promotions.

In executing promotions, Catalina operates under the assumption that the best predictor of a consumer's future behavior is their past behavior, and it tracks this behavior using the frequent shopper cards that people keep in their wallets or attached to their key chains. In explaining how the cards work, Mansfield notes that Catalina needs to balance the often-competing demands of three separate constituents: the CPG manufacturers, the grocery retailers, and consumers. He explains:

> If you have a frequent shopper card, I don't need to know who you are. All I need to know is that you've got a 16-digit card number that you scan when you go into the grocery store. Once I see that number, I can then see all of the products you bought during that transaction, and I store the information. You come in a week later, scan the card again, and now I can combine the products you bought in this transaction with the ones you bought in the previous one. I'm effectively building a longitudinal profile of you. I don't know if you are male or female. I have no idea of your household income. I don't have your address. All I know is that you are a specific 16-digit number that I can track all of the purchases against.*

While Catalina does not maintain personally identifiable information in its database, due to privacy concerns, it can nonetheless make its number-coded profiles available to the retailers who do maintain access to that information. The retailers can match the profiles up to the names and addresses of the customers who opted in to get the frequent shopper card, and proceed to market to them in a context-sensitive way.

For their part, the CPG companies can gain direct access to consumers through the company's Checkout Coupons point-of-sale systems in the stores, as we have indicated, and/or through direct mail programs. "If I'm a product manager coming out with a new cookie, what would be better than to put a product sample into the household of a heavy Chips Ahoy! user?" asks Mansfield. "Not only

---

* Ibid.

that, but then, two or three weeks later, follow up the next time one of these users comes into the store with a continuity offer."

Today, Catalina is moving beyond the grocery store aisles, and into pharmacies. The company is even testing the waters of the restaurant business, having recently piloted a program with McDonald's, using the same coupon printer technology. The goal is to give customers who dined at McDonald's for breakfast or lunch incentives to come back for dinner, by providing them with cost savings. Compare the likely outcomes of a mass marketing campaign designed to increase customer share of wallet through brand awareness ("Did somebody say McDonald's?") against that of a precision marketing campaign that puts tailored coupons into the hands of people who just paid for an actual McDonald's meal.

In measuring Marketing ROI, Catalina has essentially adopted the scientific method, which it calls "the households impact test." The idea is to match up a thousand households that have similar brand usage profiles to create a test group and a control group. Catalina will offer incentives and communications to the test households and nothing to the control households, and then follow the former over a period of three to six months to find out how their brand or category usage changed compared to the latter. "We have a very scientific method to find out whether or not we've moved the needle," says Mansfield.

THE CUSTOMER LIFE CYCLE THROUGH
THE PRECISION MARKETING LENSES

Customer relationships have a natural life cycle, much like products and services. The different stages of the customer life cycle demand different marketing strategies, and companies need to adapt their resource allocation and management tactics accordingly.[17] In addition, they need to assess the value of each relationship on an ongoing basis to determine its *option value*—that is, whether the *lifetime potential* of the relationship is such that it merits increased attention and investment.

By using the customer life cycle as a reference, marketers can also gain a better understanding for what kinds of questions they should be asking themselves (and also asking their customers), depending on which stage the relationship has progressed to—and ultimately, what kinds of returns they should expect to accrue and how to measure them. While the phases are broadly defined, what is important is that the company realizes that its strategies, its investment focus, and its metrics evolve and maintain consistency across the three stages of the customer life cycle. These stages are Attract, Retain, and Leverage, as shown in Figure 2.2.

ATTRACT: SECURE THE RELATIONSHIP

In thinking about customer attraction, it helps to take a cue from the classic 1936 book *How to Win Friends and Influence People*, a book that has sold some 15 million copies and which even today

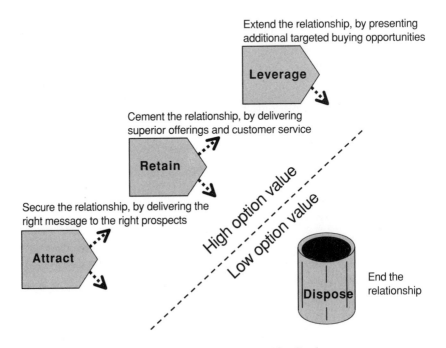

FIGURE 2.2   Stages of the Customer Life Cycle

cracks the ranks of Amazon's top 100 sellers. In the book, Dale Carnegie listed "six ways to make people like you":

1. Become genuinely interested in other people.
2. Smile.
3. Remember that a person's name is to that person the sweetest and most important sound in any language.
4. Be a good listener. Encourage others to talk about themselves.
5. Talk in terms of the other person's interests.
6. Make the other person feel important—and do it sincerely.

The rules for using precision marketing to attract new customers are much the same—especially the part about being a good listener, encouraging people to talk about themselves, responding in terms of their interests, and making them feel important. Indeed, attraction begins by knowing what drives a potential customer to action—as Dale Carnegie puts it, "arousing in them an eager want."[18]

To get there, a company needs to answer the question: "Why should customers want to do business with us?" The answer needs to be highly compelling and present a clarity of competitive position, by putting forth a precise statement of value that strongly resonates with people's wants, needs, and interests. This is the *value proposition*. Traditionally, the value proposition was defined as *a specific configuration of benefits that a company offers to a specific customer segment*. Ideally, the marketing effort would then revolve around the effort to communicate the specific configuration of benefits to the specific customer segment. But because mass media vehicles can be used only to communicate the *same* message to *all* segments, most companies would, in reality, try to highlight only benefits with the widest appeal so as to attract the largest possible number of customers.

Today, however, the combination of mass customization, product bundling, and precision marketing makes it possible for companies to tailor both their offerings and their communications to *multiple* customer segments. After all, more than one segment may be highly profitable. Yet the reason that one segment may want to do business with you may be very different from that of another segment. With the rise of precision marketing, companies can efficiently address these differences to attract customers with a broad range of wants, needs, and interests.

RETAIN: CEMENT THE RELATIONSHIP (OR DISPOSE OF IT!)

In marketing, the proof of the pudding is when customers come back for a second helping. Yet customers don't always want a second helping, and this can lead to some desperate situations. Consider the recent antics of a "new economy magazine," one that had known happier times before 2003 rolled around. That's when the subscription department mailed a series of renewal offers that resembled collection agency notices. "Delinquent Account—Immediate Action Required," the letter began. It continued: "You have been placed on our Bad Debt File" and "We were forced to pursue this course of action" and "To resolve this matter in a satisfactory fashion, it is imperative you send payment today." While some customers may have been cowed into taking out their checkbooks, such scare tactics are generally not the best way to pursue customer retention.

The retain phase focuses on keeping the *right* customer relationships. The effort may involve the need to assess the overall profitability of each customer segment, to determine the best allocation of resources. Of course, most companies have loyal customers. The problem with loyal customers, however, is that companies often know the numerator but not the denominator. In other words, they may know the *current value* of those customers to the company but not their *potential value*. Fact is, some loyal customers may be only marginally valuable today, but enormously valuable tomorrow.

Again, assigning customer value first means performing customer lifetime value calculations—that is, determining a customer's total potential value to a company over the course of his or her cumulative transactions, past, present, and *especially* future. The goal is to identify which customers are likely to be the most profitable down the road, and which should therefore be escalated to higher levels of customer care in anticipation of that future payoff.

Consider a student enrolled in a graduate school program—verification of which can be readily obtained through a precision marketing program. At this stage of his life, the student's insurance needs may be minimal. He may require nothing more than a bare-bones automobile policy. That being the case, a large, multiproduct insurance company may be disinclined to bend over backward to win his patronage. But perhaps it should. Response-based data may further indicate that his post-graduation plans include climbing the corporate ladder, in which case his insurance needs could significantly rise. Because a student's *lifetime* value may actually be very high, insurance companies (and the independent agencies that represent them) may do well to think long-term, even to the point of pricing that initial bare-bones policy as a loss leader to achieve early "lock-in." A small subsidy on the front-end could produce significant upside on the back-end. For companies with different products to sell over the life cycle of a customer relationship, the sooner the better to establish that relationship.

Finally, as we've suggested, companies need to consider the notion of "customer clearance," or disposal. In general, disposal should occur when the cost of maintaining a relationship exceeds the value derived from it, or that will likely be derived from it in the future based on option value considerations. A company should routinely purge unproductive relationships from its customer base just as it routinely purges unproductive relationships from its employee payroll. Using periodic performance reviews, companies systematically identify and dismiss underperforming employees. Why don't companies have performance reviews for customers? Why aren't underperforming customers subject to being let go?

Part of the problem is that employees are generally treated as a liability on the balance sheet while customers are generally treated as an asset. Such thinking can be erroneous—and expensive. Another, related problem is that many companies simply don't realize that some percentage of their customers are deeply unprofitable, and that doing business with them can ultimately reduce shareholder value. In fact, a recent study at Harvard Business School concludes that the least profitable 10 percent of a company's customers can lose anywhere from 50 percent to 200 percent of its total profits. Meanwhile, shattering long-held assumptions, another study shows that a company's most loyal customers may contribute almost *nothing* to its profitability. In short, corporate leaders tend to spend too much time looking at conventional operating results and not enough time looking at customer profitability. Fact is, every company has its share of deadwood. The key is to discard it, and then take the appropriate action to either divest of or invest in those customers who are on the profitability fence in terms of their lifetime value.

LEVERAGE: EXTEND THE RELATIONSHIP

A fundamental concept in physics, the principle of leverage also exists in finance, where the use of credit or borrowed funds (buying securities on margin, for example) can increase the rate of return on an investment. Leverage is equally applicable in the context of customer relationship strategy, where the emphasis shifts from cementing the relationship to broadening the breadth and depth of the relationship. Generally, this requires a deep understanding of the customer segment and the potential synergies that may exist for marketing complementary products, line extensions, and new product categories.

With leverage, the name of the game is increasing share of wallet and customer yield. So, not only do companies need to prevent attrition of profitable customers, as we've suggested, but

they also need to maximize value against those customers, by fig-
uring out what other products and services to up-sell and cross-
sell to them. Precision marketing can be used effectively in this
capacity—for example, as we discuss in the previous section, by
targeting customers based on their profit potential.

Consider an initiative recently launched by the retail and
commercial operations unit of Bridgestone/Firestone, one of the
world's largest manufacturers of tires and other rubber products.
In 2002, the unit estimated that the difference in the amount of
revenue between what its customers currently spend on automo-
tive services and what they *could* spend totals nearly $600 million.
And whereas the unit had previously allocated the bulk of its
marketing spend toward trying to derive increased value from
the top 20 percent of its customer base (customers who may, in
fact, have already been spending at their maximum levels), now
the unit has shifted gears, to focus on customers with the greatest
profit potential.[19]

How did the unit determine customer profit potential? By analyzing a number of different factors, including a customer's life
stage, marital status, and household income, as well as the age
and type of vehicle they own. Most of the vehicle information was
already available, since a majority of the 2,000-plus service outlets
track it over a period of 5 years. The information was used to determine the average spend for different types of customers with
different types of cars over different periods of time. Based on the
findings, customers were assigned to five different categories, and
then further segmented according to the amount of money they
actually spent with the company. By comparing the actual spending levels of each subsegment against its estimated total value, the
Bridgestone/Firestone unit was able to shift its customer contact
priorities. Now it targets its marketing messages to those customers with the highest revenue potential—as opposed to those
who may well spend the most money with the company but may
nonetheless have already reached their spending potential. Moreover, it sends new customers a version of the direct mail welcome

package tailored to their probable spending level. So much for the standard, one-size-fits-all welcome packages of the past.

USING PRECISION MARKETING
TO INFLUENCE THE INFLUENCERS

Nowhere is the dynamic of leverage more evident than in the world of avid moviegoers. Hollywood's most effective marketing tool—albeit one it has no direct control over—can be summarized in the form of a question: "Seen any good movies lately?" Rave reviews by fastidious friends can have an enormous impact on how well a movie performs, potentially allowing one that did poorly in the opening weekend to quickly reverse course. (In fact, two economists—Arthur De Vany and W. David Walls—have found that positive word of mouth is the *only* real determinant of a movie's long-term success.)

A perfect example is *My Big Fat Greek Wedding*, a star-deficient, little-heralded film that cost a scant $5 million to make. It opened in April 2002. Still playing in theaters a year later, *Greek Wedding* was by far the most profitable independent movie ever made, grossing more than $240 million at the box office. Britain's indie hit *Bend It Like Beckham*, which took just eight weeks and $4.5 million to make, enjoyed a similar, if much smaller, trajectory the following year, also on the power of old-fashioned word of mouth.

Of course the principle that applies to movies also applies to the launch of every product and service. Intuit's Quicken software, which quickly reached $33 million in annual sales, grew largely through positive word of mouth. Starbucks, whose humble beginnings include giving away coffee samples at Seattle's Pikes Place Market, also owes much of its early success to the network effects of personal recommendations. In the early days of eBay, as many as 50 percent of new members were enrolled via referrals. Or to take a more mundane example, consider the Swiffer. Launched by P&G in 1999 as a broom alternative, the Swiffer and its accessory products took only four years to generate more than $350 million in sales, thanks largely to the free marketing enacted by passionate customers.

Remember that 1970s TV advertisement in which an attractive young model waves her lustrous hair while elucidating the reason for the growing popularity of Faberge shampoo? "I told two friends," she says, "and they told two friends, and *they* told two friends. . . ." Today, network technology can take the process of friends telling friends to a whole new level, dramatically speeding it up and expanding its scale and scope. It can enable satisfied customers to spread the word about a product or service instantaneously and en masse through the magic of so-called viral marketing—commonly defined as digitally augmented word of mouth. To some extent, marketers can facilitate the process—for example, by including a simple message at the end of a sweepstakes registration: "Thanks for entering. Now, go tell your friends." And then, of course, giving them an easy way to do so by providing electronic invitations they can send, as well as other brand promotion vehicles, such as postcards, screensavers, and game pieces that can be easily forwarded and shared. Some electronic coupon programs provide existing customers with cash incentives for referring new customers and encouraging them to shop.

Of course, the flip side of positive word of mouth is negative word of mouth, which can also spread like wildfire, with detrimental consequences for the object of derision. Moreover, negative word of mouth tends to be far more prevalent than positive word of mouth, with studies suggesting that people are anywhere from 3 to 10 times more likely to tell others about a negative experience than a positive one. While the propensity for people to accentuate the negative no doubt reveals some larger truths about our culture from a sociological perspective, looking at the phenomenon from a business perspective also makes for some fascinating observations.

A vivid portrait of how negative word of mouth can rapidly proliferate via e-mail can be found in the now-famous PowerPoint presentation Yours is a Very Bad Hotel. Created by two would-be guests of a Houston-area hotel, the "graphic complaint" documents their experiences after being refused rooms for which they held confirmed reservations. Replete with a two-by-two matrix that plots the hotel's standard of service delivery against a Taliban-run hostel in Kabul, Afghanistan, the grievances take on a no-holds-barred life of their own. Originally sent in late 2001 to a handful of friends, the e-mail attachment was forwarded hundreds of thousands of times within the span of a few months, along the way doing untold damage to the hotel's reputation.

Or consider the story of former M.I.T. graduate student Jonah Peretti who, also in 2001, sent a few of his friends an e-mail exchange he had had with a customer service rep at Nike iD, an online service that allows customers to personalize their Nike running shoes. Peretti had chosen the word "sweatshop," and Nike had promptly cancelled the order. An amusing and provocative discussion ensued. A spoof of an ad for another sneaker company—PUMA—offers a more recent example of how brand-related material can very quickly become "the talk of the Internet."

In fact, mock ads for all kinds of brands, from Budweiser to Levi's, have recently generated a tremendous amount of buzz on the Internet, particularly by a young, highly coveted generation of consumers who tend to be nonresponsive to conventional advertising. This has led many observers to conclude that the ads may actually benefit the very brands they aim to spoof. *Subviral marketing*, as the phenomenon is called, is proving to be an effective way to drive brand awareness—and who knows, some of the mock ads may even be inside jobs. Why not? After all, it costs nothing to let people forward mock ads via e-mail, which is hardly the case when it comes to airing real ads on prime-time TV.

"Micromedia has the potential to reach just as many people as mass media," notes Peretti, whose Nike discussion helped set the trend. "Most e-mail forwards die before they are widely distributed, but if critical mass is attained, it is possible to reach millions of people without spending any money at all."[20] In addition to being forwarded around the world via e-mail, the Nike discussion was posted on shey.net, an early weblog, or blog, where it gained even wider exposure. These days, blogs are the most potent form of buzz generator around. By allowing nonjournalists to become curators of annotated links, blogs help democratize the dissemination of people's opinions about anything and everything. In the context of precision marketing, the question becomes: How can a company identify people who are most likely to create positive word of mouth, and then allocate a portion of its marketing spend toward facilitating their efforts? The answer may be worth more than a national media buy—and maybe even the naming rights to a sports arena.

Of course, certain people naturally wield a disproportionate degree of influence over what other people think, do, and say, as well as what they buy. This is no recent revelation; in exploring the way opinions and attitudes spread, researchers Paul Lazarsfeld and Elihu Katz came to the same conclusion in the 1940s. More recently, in 2003, two Roper Polls veterans—Ed Keller and Jon Barry—published a book provocatively entitled *The Influentials: One American in Ten Tells the Other Nine How to Vote, Where to Eat, and What to Buy*. The authors present no shortage of empirical data to support their bold assertions regarding the Ten Percent Influentials Club—a club that also applies to the younger set, according to Teenage Research Unlimited (TRU). "Over the past 20 years, we've evolved our own segmentation scheme based on trend adoption," explains Peter Zollo, TRU's president and founder (and a man *BusinessWeek* dubbed "the teenage marketing guru"). According to the TRU scheme, which divides teens into four unique groups, the "Influencer" category—those kids whom the wannabes want to be—do make up only about 10 percent of the teen population. "That's actually good news for marketers who want to reach a mass audience," explains Zollo. "We've learned that targeting Influencers is the most effective way to reach about 80 percent of all teens." Zollo notes that mass marketers often target marketing programs to the largest teen group—what TRU calls "the Conformers." But this is all wrong.

"Conformers are always looking up the curve," says Zollo. "They aspire to be Influencers, and so that's where they take their cues, from fashion to food."[21]

All of which, again, begs the question: To what extent can the so-called Influencers be identified and segmented as discrete population groups, such that companies can reach out to them, connect with them, and potentially recruit them as part of their overall marketing efforts? Is advance "positive word-of-mouth segmentation" really possible? And if so, what kind of demographic, attitudinal, or behavioral response data do companies need to capture using precision marketing techniques in order to identify and target the ones-who-beget-the-tens (the so-called "key multipliers")? And once identified, how can companies then entice and enlist these individuals to spread their messages, using the Internet as a mechanism for leverage—enabling them, like the ancient Greek scholar Archimedes, to lift loads well beyond their natural capacity?

We don't know the answer—although Google's recent acquisition of Blogger.com, the leading blog publishing service, may provide a clue to at least one piece of the puzzle. Imagine applying Google's targeted advertising and online profiling capabilities, as discussed in the previous chapter, in the context of an Influencer's blog page. A blogger writes an entry to document a recent sneaker-buying expedition. Readers view the entry, and suddenly an ad for Nike basketball pops up on the screen. The ad is context-sensitive—and implicitly endorsed by an Influencer! But alas, would the community of bloggers ever allow such a blatantly commercial thing to happen to their personal message boards? Could a reciprocal value exchange be structured that would permit the possible inclusion of paid advertising—or would bloggers forever regard this virtual real estate transaction as an untenable compromise to their artistic integrity? Like most crazy ideas related to marketing, only time will tell.

3
EXPLOITING THE DATA

You can count the number of seeds in an apple, but you can't count the number of apples in a seed.

—Ken Kesey

The British geneticist R.A. Fisher once remarked: "To call in the statistician after the experiment is done may be no more than asking him to perform a post-mortem examination; he may be able to say what the experiment died of." More than half a century later as we consider the subject of customer data management and predictive analytics, Fisher's words are perhaps more relevant than ever.

To improve the effectiveness of their marketing expenditures, companies must exploit their stores of customer data—and, ideally, this means calling in the statistician while the experiment is still alive. As we suggest in previous chapters, companies should embrace the notion of active experimentation on an ongoing basis as a way to optimize the value of their data, ultimately leading to better marketing decisions—and an overall competitive advantage.

If only it were that simple. Although the challenges for marketers are many, they all seem to stem from four fundamental failings:

~ Inability to capture relevant data
~ Inability to integrate the data
~ Inability to understand the data
~ Inability to apply the data

"The low-hanging fruit for marketing improvement is a better understanding of the data," notes Mike Duffy, the head of customer analytics at Kraft Foods, articulating a view held by customer analytics directors across the corporate landscape.[1] Invariably, this better understanding of the data comes from the application of various mathematical analytical techniques. We've already mentioned a few of them: correlation analysis, discriminant analysis, cluster analysis, regression analysis, neural nets, genetic algorithms, and the list goes on. Some of these techniques are new to the consumer marketing arena—but not necessarily new to other business processes or areas of discipline, such as the life sciences and artificial intelligence—while some have been practiced by traditional direct marketers for decades in their relentless efforts to translate customer information into more effective marketing campaigns.

Gartner defines analytics as "the technology area that applies mathematical transformations to data and previous insights to produce new insights." In our view, analytics is simply a business intelligence tool that marketers can use to answer the question "so what?" It provides a sense-making framework that can shine light on a company's terabytes of customer data and the hundreds of different variables that may be embedded in that data. It informs the segmentation schemes that may then spring forth from that data and—most importantly—the best potential marketing treatments (and the most appropriate service levels) that the company may then wish to pursue for each different segment, given the overall business objectives.

Success in marketing analytics is largely a function of both the quality and quantity of the data—which, after all, serves as the raw material from which the new insights are formed. "For us, the big opportunity is in improving the quality of our data," says Bill Mirbach, vice president of direct marketing at Intuit, articulating another commonly held view. "We're spending a lot of time right now increasing the depth of our customer knowledge, by making sure that our databases are accurate."[2]

By "accurate," Mirbach means that all of the interaction and transaction data sources, including the company's call centers, sales force automation (SFA) applications, enterprise resource planning (ERP) systems, and e-commerce/Web click-stream applications, should be fully integrated (preferably, in real time) across the entire organization, that the data should be consistent in format and cleansed of errors, and that it should follow the same set of business rules. In addition, the data may need to be optimized for analysis, and accessible in such a way that it meets the needs of the team conducting the analysis. All in all, it's just a matter of implementing the principles of good customer data management.

Unfortunately, when it comes to implementing even the most rudimentary principles of good customer data management, most companies are less enlightened than Intuit, and many still live in the proverbial Dark Ages. The reasons for their failures vary. Budgetary constraints around capital expenditures account for some of the delay. The crowded and confusing customer relationship vendor market space has perhaps provided more roadblocks than roadways for some. And the common management myopia that accompanied the late millennium boom allowed many companies to simply ignore the many gasps and groans from their sagging infrastructures, at least until the bottom fell out. The end result is as it ever was: There are a whole lot of senior managers with precious little solid ground under their feet.

There are many reasons why companies have not successfully embraced and implemented the technical infrastructures, business processes, and organizational controls necessary to exploit their burgeoning data stores. But there is really only one way out of the dilemma: Embark on a singular mission to capture and integrate relevant customer data, as prerequisites to implementing the analytical marketing solutions that can drive increased business value.

No excuses. And no time to waste. Here's how to do it.

STORMING THE BASTILLE OF CUSTOMER DATA

The mission begins by addressing the problem of isolated data silos. It's a problem that nearly every large company faces to some degree. Simply put, the problem relates to the fact that many large companies have embraced a blueprint for data management that resembles nothing more than a penitentiary, rife with walls and divisions.

One divider wall is the channel through which a customer makes a purchase. Another divider wall is the channel through which a customer obtains information or resolves a problem. Yet another divider wall is the business unit or product division from which a customer makes a purchase. In many cases, the data generated behind any one of these walls would seem destined to remain there indefinitely, confined to data warehouse prison cells that never "talk" to one another. Meanwhile, much of the data that *ought* to be generated as a result of the various interactions and transactions that take place between companies and their customers is not being captured or stored at all, in *any* data warehouse.

Organizational disparities abound. Some product divisions may capture data better than other product divisions. Some channels may capture data better than other channels. For example, customer service queries contained in an analog communication such as a fax are unlikely to be captured electronically. In many cases, the same can be said for conversations that take place with a CSR at a call center. Even data that exists in electronic format, such as an e-mail or SMS message, can sometimes fall between the cracks.

On the one hand, you've got solitary confinement. On the other hand, you've got anarchy. Neither are sustainable propositions.

It all adds up to a fractured view of the customer relationship, resulting in missed opportunities to boost customer retention, sales revenues, and profitability. After all, without the unification of customer data, a company can never know how much money an individual customer spends across all of its product divisions, making it impossible to accurately project lifetime value. In addition, without access to a holistic view of that customer's purchase history, a company may be prevented from applying the analytics that would allow it to know which products and services to cross-sell and up-sell. A single customer might appear as four or five different people, simply because the transactions and interactions with that customer are stored separately across four or five different data-capture environments. As a result, he or she might receive offers from four or five different product groups, all at the same time. To make matters worse, multiple accounts owned by different members of the same family are often treated as separate customers—the so-called *house-holding problem*—leading to even more redundant mailings, extra costs, and headaches for both the company and the customer.

Therefore, a key milestone in the evolution in customer relationship management is the advent of integrated solutions that are channel agnostic, providing a company with a single holistic view of the customer, regardless of their channel preferences. Without such solutions in place, customers will continue to endure a succession of frustrations as they interact with the company—presales, sales, and post-sales. These negative experiences are bound to pile up quickly. Meanwhile, the company will remain hamstrung in its efforts to develop a complete model of customer behavior, an integrated customer contact strategy, and a 360-degree view of its individual customer relationships.

SYNC OR SINK: INTEGRATING CUSTOMER DATA

How do you prevent profitable customers from leaving? Allocate resources toward becoming *customer-centric*—to use a term that has enjoyed a massive resurgence in popularity, even though its popularity should never have waned in the first place. As we suggested, becoming customer-centric—which practically every company now claims to be, despite the reality of the situation—requires organizations to connect their data silos so that relationship-related information can flow effortlessly between them. It also speaks to the need to create a unified *customer relationship repository* (CRR), also known as a *client information file* or *data warehouse*, to store the information.

As the central memory of a company, the CRR records information about every customer interaction in a single physical database—or in a virtually integrated environment that pulls together the information from across the entire enterprise. Gartner defines customer data integration as the combination of technology, software, processes, and services required to achieve a single, accurate, and complete view of the customer across multiple sources of customer data (internal and external), databases, and business lines. But while this definition may be satisfying in its succinctness, the implementation process itself tends to be time consuming and difficult to achieve. Indeed, the consolidation of customer information from across multiple sources generally translates into a major undertaking, one that spans the entire enterprise. "It's a corporate-wide root canal," remarked one executive. In fact, the sheer size, complexity, and expense of the undertaking, as well as the monumental disruption that it tends to cause, can be downright staggering.

Consider one such initiative currently underway at MetLife, the $32.5 billion financial services company. When completed, at a cost of more than $50 million, the initiative will deliver one of the largest systems ever built for enabling a holistic view of customer relationships. By 2010, the system is expected to house data for upward of 100 million customers, allowing employees (more than 46,000, in the case of MetLife, including 5 CIOs!) to view customer relationships across the entire company. In other words, this is no minor project. It's akin to raising your house into the air in order to pour a new foundation under it, then setting it back down again.

Microsoft offers another shining example of a company in the throes of customer data integration. For Microsoft, the early stages of the initiative meant collecting customer data from all of its legacy databases—some 25 million records, in total, including product registrations, online sign-ups, and newsletter subscriptions. Also included in the massive heap were 75 million transaction records, with an additional two thousand records being added every day. With the data integration effort well beyond the scope of a simple merge/purge process, Microsoft utilized a customer data integration (CDI) system that employs advanced algorithms to match multiple source files with single-instance reference files in order to generate a unique, persistent identifier for each individual customer. This identifier then travels with the individual customer from that point forward, making it easy to maintain a current and accurate view of the relationship. In 2002, the newly centralized CRR drove 30 marketing campaigns a month, generating $24 million in revenues (twice the original goal), allowing the initiative to quickly pay for itself.

Three years into the data integration effort, Microsoft still has a way to go before its mission is accomplished. For example, it has yet to create real-time data connectivity with its call centers and wireless touchpoints. So, while "one face, one voice" may be an attractive marketing slogan, the challenge of getting to this level of data integration can be daunting. Again, the difficulty stems in large part from the fact that the different databases within a company, as well those outside of the company, tend to rely on disparate types of languages, platforms, and architectures—not to mention the resistance in the silos that the initiative is likely to encounter.

A basic rule of thumb: The deeper the level of integration required, the greater the risk that the initiative will run into implementation hurdles. In other words, integration risk is a function of the number of integration points that exist, and the likely level of difficulty that each of them poses. The risk tends to run especially high when, as is the case with MetLife, the company is a conglomerate whose rapid growth was fueled through acquisitions. Having acquired dozens of businesses, both large and small, in its quest to build the nation's largest insurance company, MetLife eventually found itself saddled with a host of dissimilar IT systems, each of which housed mountains of invaluable but incompatible data. A bunch of businesses cobbled together can only mean stockpiles of customer data sitting across multiple pieces of the company—and a need to connect these stockpiles.

On the positive side, a company faced with widespread fragmentation of its IT systems can breathe a sigh of relief, given that there may be a viable alternative to hauling away all of the pieces, and then replacing them with one giant, unified system. The company may not even need to physically connect the pieces. Instead, it may be possible to deploy a small army of middleware solutions to do the work. These solutions are rapidly evolving, and fast becoming the answer to every CIO's prayers, as well as the answer to those of every marketing manager.

At their core, middleware solutions are designed to extract data from legacy databases, regardless of where and in what format the data is stored. The applications allow an IT system to map to the data structures where the information already resides, creating a real-time copy, as opposed to forcing all information to reside on a common data structure. In effect, they pull copies of the data from incompatible legacy databases—in the case of MetLife, they number more than 30—into a common pool that speaks a common language. In many cases, companies can integrate their data via separate application systems, each managing a separate portion of the overall "federated database," to create the illusion of unification. A benefit of the illusion is that it can extend the life of the legacy systems by orders of magnitude, saving the company millions of dollars.

So, by building bridges across silos, and funneling all data traffic through a CDI access ramp, a company may be able to create a single view of its customer relationships without having to discard any portion of its existing systems. Think of middleware solutions as serotonin for the corporate organization. A nerve chemical messenger, serotonin in the brain is passed from one nerve cell to the next through synapses. In people suffering from depressive disorders, selective serotonin reuptake inhibitors work by enabling nerve cells to communicate with one another. By the same token, middleware solutions work by enabling data silos to communicate with one another—in most cases, by using XML as the data exchange protocol. If not for these solutions, many companies would stand to become clinically depressed, at least where shareholder value is concerned!

For MetLife, the serotonin came in the form of an application from DWL, just one of many software vendors that have sprung up over the past few years promising to unify customer information across all business lines, channels, and systems in real time. According to DWL, the solution adopted by MetLife capitalizes on its existing technology by adding "a unified business service layer that sits over product-focused back office systems and CRM applications to add rich customer management functionality, cascade updates across all systems in real time, and provide a single source of customer information and administration to all."

Rather than delve into the nuts and bolts of the systems architecture or its implementation—which, as we've said, is a topic better left to another book—it's important to simply realize that the ability to propagate a current, consistent, and comprehensive view of a customer relationship to the furthermost reaches of the organization is now highly feasible and readily available to any company willing to take the leap. There are many ways across this river of integration. And the time for dangling toes in the water has passed. Choose your best vehicle and start paddling, pedaling, or swimming.

MetLife is in up to their neck, and they couldn't be happier about it. This "comprehensive view" they're working toward means that, for the first time in the company's 135-year history, a CSR in the call center can gain real-time, simultaneous access to a customer's retirement account, auto insurance policy, and dental plan, even though these three products are provided by three distinct business units. The ability to integrate both recent and in-session customer data from multiple touchpoints, and tie it all together with incoming and outgoing channels, also sets the stage for predictive analytics, as we discuss later in this chapter.

We call the task of achieving full data integration *SiloSync*. The process of gluing together pairs of applications with middleware can be arduous, and CDI success often depends on creative work-around solutions that are less than elegant from an interoperability perspective. Yet SiloSync generally leads to greater levels of customer satisfaction and many new opportunities to attract, retain, and leverage profitable customers. Again, think of it as a prerequisite to the optimization of marketing, sales, and customer care functions, and a critical step in the never-ending struggle to keep good customers from buying competitive products or services.

SiloSync tears down the boundaries that separate channels, geographies, and business units. It connects disparate parts of a company, as well as selected partners and suppliers across the extended business network, allowing them to gain access to a current, consistent, and comprehensive view of any customer relationship. Importantly, in the context of precision marketing, it links all marketing, sales, and customer service processes to an integrated infrastructure comprised of multiple software applications. We call this infrastructure a *customer-facing applications suite* (CFAS). We regard it with a sense of awe, knowing that it holds the key to the future of precision marketing.

DEVELOPING A CUSTOMER DATA ASSET

With a robust set of information, a customer database can be a company's richest asset. Such a data model takes time and effort to create. In fact, the job is never finished, as the data should be constantly updated, cleansed, and carefully maintained like any other critical and highly valuable information asset. Best practices for creating and maintaining a consumer-centric marketing database include four primary steps:

Consolidating Current Data Feeds. Customer data comes from many online and offline sources—website registrations, bingo cards, customer call centers, retail loyalty card information, and so on. These data sources must be consolidated into a single data warehouse that represents one view of the customer.

Cleaning Data. The various sources of information may conflict or be ambiguous. Is Mr. Bill Weingarten at 1102 Pratt the same as Mr. William Weingarten @ 1102 W. Pratt? The first step in cleansing involves cleaning up contact information based on postal codes and data hygiene software. In addition, data fields may have been constructed differently. For example, a brand website may have the field "age" with choices listed as 1 = 18–25; 2 = 26–40; 3 = 41+; in a registration card, the field "age" may have choices listed as 1 = 18–25; 2 = 36–55; 3 = 56+. These discrepancies must be reconciled in a transformation process.

Gaining Permission. Customers must opt in and give permission to marketers to communicate with them. Managing the opportunities to opt in (or out) across multiple channels and communications requires establishment of clear business rules. In addition, customers must have explicit privacy policies, which they enforce (e.g., Safe Harbor certification to ensure consumer trust).

Enriching Profiles. A profile enrichment strategy includes what information the company can obtain about its customers and from which sources. That information must be more valuable than nice-to-know. It must be useful in some way, whether by feeding predictive modeling, identifying influencers, or driving campaign personalization. This data can be enriched in three ways:

Purchasing Data Overlays: Large database marketing vendors can append data to individual consumer profiles, based on variables from within their own databases. These firms can also provide data hygiene services.

Asking Consumers Directly: Interactions with consumers (e.g., at registration, entry into a sweepstakes) provide opportunities to obtain personal information. Small surveys that build profiles over time are an excellent way of gathering meaningful data.

Imputation: Based on statistical modeling techniques, statisticians infer the value of a particular data field based on similar consumers' responses.

CREATING THE CUSTOMER-FACING APPLICATIONS SUITE (CFAS)

The customer relationship repository constitutes the heart of the customer-facing applications suite. No other technology component plays a more critical role in fueling a company's journey toward becoming customer-centric. At the same time, the CRR accounts for only one piece of the CFAS—again, an acronym that we use to describe the end-to-end set of technology components that a company employs so as to better understand its customers, more effectively go to market with its offerings, and build more profitable customer relationships. In an ideal world, the CFAS should contain all of the enabling technology that a company requires, such that every customer interaction can be captured, monitored, and analyzed in a consistent fashion to progressively improve customer satisfaction and overall profitability.

Taken as a whole, the CFAS spans the marketing activities that precede the transaction, the sales activities that consummate the transaction, and the support activities that follow the transaction. It also spans a diverse set of channels that a company may use to connect with its customers. Embedded within the CFAS are the operational aspects of interacting and transacting with customers, as well as the analytical aspects of segmentation strategy and predictive modeling to improve the profitability of customer relationships. The CFAS should enable a company to evolve its customer interactions from fragmented silos of activities and information to an integrated solution that spans all transaction and communication channels, including those managed by external partners.

A full-fledged CFAS is comprised of three main elements of functionality, in addition to the CRR that houses the relationship data.[3] These elements are: the *campaign manager*, the *channel manager*, and a set of analytical tools that collectively we call the *analytics manager*, as shown in Figure 3.1. Taken together, these three elements of functionality translate into the "killer app" of marketing optimization, and the intelligent machinery that enables precision marketing.

If the CRR serves as the record keeper of customer data, then the campaign manager serves as the choreographer of customer interactions. It is the combined set of tools that allows a company to categorize and profile its customers, design customized mar-

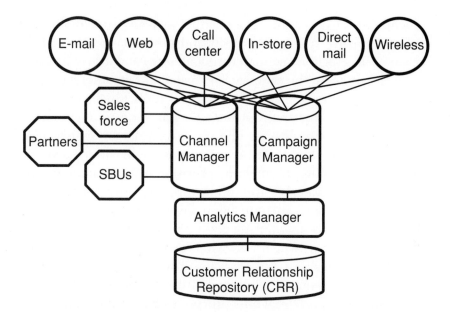

FIGURE 3.1   The Customer-Facing Applications Suite (CFAS)

keting campaigns, and evaluate the performance of marketing
programs. The campaign manager also tracks each customer's
past purchase behavior and stated communication preferences,
to allow marketers to present future offers through the touchpoints to which they are most likely to respond, be it by direct
mail, e-mail, phone, text messaging, and so on.

At the same time that the campaign manager is tracking purchase behavior and communication preferences, the channel
manager is doing its job, which is to connect the various touchpoints for customer interaction—linking, for example, to the
sales force automation system, the call center (in-sourced *or* outsourced), and the Internet-based customer interaction channels.
Ideally, the channel manager integrates *all* customer interaction
and transaction data across *all* channels for use throughout *all*
parts of the extended business network. It captures information
from every customer touchpoint, transfers the information to the
CRR, and retrieves outputs from the analytics modules to every

touchpoint for execution. The channel manager should also enable a company to view the activity and performance of all of its customer interaction channels simultaneously and in real time.

As mentioned, the campaign manager and channel manager are complemented by a set of analytical tools which, again, we simply refer to as the analytics manager. Forever evolving in terms of scope and sophistication, the tools are used to analyze customer data to identify patterns, to interpret these patterns, and to then use the findings to fine-tune precision marketing programs. The tools are invaluable for sifting through large quantities of data in an automated and efficient manner—the so-called process of *data mining*—to discover nuggets of insight. Traditionally, analytics has been performed as a batch process, meaning that the analysis of results and the adaptation of campaigns have been conducted in a sequential manner. Today, however, analytics has begun to evolve into a real-time process, with execution, optimization, and adaptation becoming part of a continuous, automated loop that mirrors the Precision Marketing Cycle outlined in the previous chapter.

Also, as we've said, marketing decisions in the past have tended to be driven in large measure by intuition, perception, and a sixth sense—in short, the opposite of the scientific method. In contrast, the analytics manager relies almost entirely on mathematical modeling techniques, enabling it to make decisions *more* rationally and *less* by gut instinct, and evolve its marketing treatment and resource allocation processes from ones that are judgment-based to ones that are fact-based and that promote financial accountability. The move from "subjective decision-making" to "objective decision-making" represents a dramatic improvement over the way marketing programs have traditionally been run.

Making "objective decision-making" part of the marketing process may seem like a radical concept, until one stops to consider the fact that most other technology-enabled business processes in a company already adhere to an extensive set of *business rules*, implemented by specialized software applications known as *business rules engines*. Today, most large companies have thousands of business rules driving their core business processes. These business rules reflect the company's decision-making logic—and, to a certain extent, dictate its overall behavior.

Until recently, a company's business rules had to be hard-coded deep inside its operational systems. Changing a rule meant recoding the software, a time-consuming task only programmers could perform. Today, however, a new breed of decision-making technologies is allowing nonprogrammers to automate business processes by letting them write and modify the rules themselves. This is important, since the rules are subject to continuous change, due to an ever-expanding universe of variables.

Put simply, a business rule determines what actions to take based on the set of variables contained within a conditional statement. For example: If field $A = X$, then perform B given variable X and constraint Y. Translated into the language of precision marketing, the business rule might read: If Customer Segment A responds in the affirmative to questions 1, 2, and 5 on the online response form, then perform Marketing Treatment B to those members of the segment who live in the Pacific Northwest and who don't already own a sports utility vehicle. Business rules technology is a fundamental component of enterprise decision management. And, in many ways, an analytics manager is exactly that: a business rules engine, with many of the rules guided by predictive models, as we discuss later in this chapter.

In summary, an integrated set of customer-facing applications starts with the customer relationship repository, and is complemented by three key sets of operational applications: the campaign manager for marketing activities, the channel manager for customer interactions, and the analytics manager for querying, analysis, and reporting of customer data. There are many roads to creating the CFAS—including outsourcing it altogether. For each of these roads, however, the goal is the same: better management of the company's most important asset—its customer information.

CRAFTING A VALUE-BASED DIALOGUE

Think of the many messages that compete for consumers' attention in a given day. Of the hundreds of e-mails, direct mail solicitations, telemarketing calls, billboards, magazine ads, and so on they experience each day, which get even a fraction of their attention? Which entice them to offer information about themselves? Only those that offer sufficient value warrant giving personal information as an equitable exchange. Creating such a dialogue with consumers and the resulting opportunity to sell requires discipline in three key areas:

1. Opportunities to engage.
2. Experimentation.
3. Measurement.

Opportunities to Engage. Opportunities to engage in a dialogue with consumers typically occur in these ways:

Event-driven (e.g., a winter storm triggers an e-mailed recipe for a hot beverage)

Demographics-based (e.g., a free pamphlet on puberty mailed to mothers of teens)

Purchasing information-based (e.g., promoting a dry cleaning store in the same mall where a particular consumer buys groceries)

Curriculum-based (e.g., offering a series of educational e-mails on healthy eating for runners or senior citizens)

Experimentation. All brand managers have experienced the difficulty of choosing among campaign possibilities. The variables that could affect response are endless: content, subject line, graphics, price point, bundling, and so on. A good campaign management tool allows for sophisticated experimentation to test the effects of a variety of attributes on the desired response. Testing and measuring results before implementing full campaigns, and then using these results to create predictive models, enable companies to accurately predict response rates and costs. Using these tools, marketers can determine where to invest their precious marketing dollars.

Measurement. Tracking results of a single campaign is not enough. Marketing managers need to be able to see the value of a series of campaigns over time. Careful definition of the metrics for measuring the campaign or series of campaigns must drive how the data is displayed. Further, easy-to-understand reports or results-displaying "dashboards" are essential to a well-managed precision marketing program.

FROM MARKETING AUTOMATION
TO MARKETING OPTIMIZATION

The terms *automatic pilot, automatic transmission,* and *automatic washing machine* (and countless others that share the same common denominator) conjure up images of mechanical devices operating with minimal human intervention. Push a button, and let the machine do the rest. Yet, interestingly, the word *automate,* from the Greek word *automatos,* meaning "acting of one's own will," was originally used to describe qualities endemic to living organisms—the "automatic digestion" of food, for example. According to *The American Heritage Dictionary,* the association of the word *automate* with computers and machinery "may represent one instance of many in which we have come to see the world in mechanical terms."

139

Certainly, the term *marketing automation* describes a technology-enabled process insofar as it refers to the electronic execution of marketing programs through the use of data mining techniques. Again, these techniques are used to identify patterns that can be used in support of designing the right offers and formulating the right messages for narrow customer segments. Meanwhile, reporting tools are used to analyze the results of past or current marketing campaigns, allowing companies to fine-tune the execution of future marketing campaigns. Unlike the batch mode process that characterized the planning and execution of traditional marketing programs in years past, marketing automation allows campaigns to be designed, executed, and adapted in real-time.

With the rise of *marketing optimization*, companies can exert even greater amounts of control over the business outcomes of their marketing programs. For instance, they can define their specific marketing goals (e.g., increased customer relationship profitability or reduced customer acquisition cost), as well as the constraints of their marketing campaigns (e.g., budget limitations or product-specific volume requirements). Predictive modeling can then determine the relative propensity of each customer segment to respond to certain promotions, while optimization algorithms can determine the best possible matches among customer segments, product offers, and marketing channels.

Ideally, a company can know, in advance, the maximum profit that can be achieved by a multi-offer marketing campaign operating within any given set of constraints, resulting in a precision marketing program that promises to deliver optimal performance. And today, with companies under pressure to cut costs and boost profitability, the words "optimal performance" should be music to anybody's ears.

After all, what company *doesn't* want to know the best mix of product offers to send to each customer segment so as to meet or exceed its sales goals? Or the efficacy of sending one customer segment a product offer through, say, an outbound e-mail campaign while presenting a different segment with a different product offer through, say, the call center? Marketing optimization promises to dramatically improve the productivity of a company's marketing-related investments, even while meeting multiple (sometimes conflicting) business goals. The key to fulfilling this promise lies largely in the ability to engage in active experimentation.

Using advanced experimental design techniques, analysts can toy with all of the different variables related to a specific marketing program. Basically, this involves testing a number of multiple feature combinations, and then applying a methodology called *fractional factorial analysis* to break down the results to determine which factors influenced which results. The idea is to create a working template that allows marketers to pick and choose the most effective feature combinations across all of the different customer segments. The ongoing cycle of testing, learning, building models, and collecting data again echoes the Precision Marketing Cycle. Certainly, it provides a systematic approach far superior to past practices, which usually involved testing only one factor at a time for only one segment at a time. By engaging in active experimentation, Marketing ROI becomes an upfront exercise rather than a post-mortem one.

"Well, great!" exclaims an enthusiastic CEO who, having heard the pitch, is sold on the idea that marketing optimization could be the ticket to increased shareholder value. "I'll take it." Which begs the question: Take *what*? Where does one go to find a fully integrated CFAS architecture, complete with the aforementioned experimental design capability? Is there an off-the-shelf, plug-and-play version just waiting to be shipped? Wishful thinking. In reality, no single software vendor, and no single set of software applications, offer all elements of marketing optimization functionality due to the diverse nature of the applications involved in the end-to-end process. Furthermore, marketing optimization is as much a service as it is a product. It relies not only on software applications but also, just as importantly, on a team of human beings with specialized expertise. In terms of the software, most large companies would need to cobble together their CFAS architecture by starting with a core platform from one of the leading vendors, then layering on additional best-of-breed components, integrated using middleware applications. Complete marketing optimization solutions may still be years away, and even then will require large capital investments in both people and infrastructure to bring them to life.

This kind of component-based, best-of-breed environment resembles nothing if not the world of high-end home theater. Sure, you can purchase an all-in-one, theater-in-a-box system. And for the average guy or gal looking to watch Simpsons DVDs, maybe that's good enough. But for the true film aficionado—or for the high-performance marketer for whom mediocre results simply are not acceptable—this is not an option. The aficionado enjoys the work it takes to build his system, to select and place the speakers that best combine performance and aesthetics, and to measure which vendor's lasers are best equipped to discover and unleash the real warmth behind digitally encoded ones and zeros.

This is not to say that owning a fully integrated, high performance CFAS is impossible. It's not. But only the richest companies, those that place an almost eccentric premium on customer centricity, will do so. The rest of us will do what we do when we visit a first-rate movie theater: We'll borrow them. More about that in the next chapter.

For now, suffice it to say that the combination of marketing automation and optimization represents a quantum leap in marketing effectiveness. It allows customer interactions to evolve from a batch process to a real-time process, and from a single-product, single-channel process to a multiple-product, multi-channel process. It also allows customization to be carried out at a narrow segment level, based on the commonalities of customer profile information. The ability to create customized marketing programs adapted to customer characteristics, behaviors, and circumstances describes the very essence of marketing optimization—and precision marketing, in particular.

PREDICTIVE MODELING: THE MAGIC 8 BALL
FOR BUILDING CUSTOMER RELATIONSHIPS

Most of the marketing messages that are communicated to consumers using mass media vehicles go to waste. So, too, does most of the information that is captured about consumers using database marketing techniques go to waste. In fact, the vast majority of the world's information that has been collected about consumers is sitting dormant on terabyte hard drives—and, even worse, in massive file cabinets. It's unorganized. It's "uncleansed." It's chock-full of redundancies and format inconsistencies. It's partially obsolete. It's pockmarked with billions of gaping holes indicating missing data fields. Still, it's there. What's lacking is the ability—and perhaps the inclination, as well—to complete, manipulate, and analyze the voluminous data and turn it into true insights that can help companies to drive revenues and margins.

The idea of turning a company's mountains of customer data into "true insight" underlies a key concept known as *predictive modeling*. The term holds enormous sway in the realm of competitive strategy, as it can be a decisive factor in boosting a company's financial performance and market value. This fact has been shown countless times across many industries—most notably, perhaps, in the area of financial services. We should know. After all, Fair Isaac pioneered the use of predictive models to assess credit risk ("credit scoring"), beginning in the 1950s. Today, the company's FICO scores are fundamental to most lending decisions. All told, Fair Isaac has developed thousands of models—for predicting attrition, bankruptcy, propensity to buy, revenue fraud, underwriting loss, loan prepayment, and so on.

Predictive modeling involves looking at large quantities of historic data, with the help of data mining tools that search for meaningful patterns, and then creating mathematical equations that represent the underlying relationships within that data. These mathematical equations are designed to forecast future behaviors. Once built, a predictive model can instantly execute a complex analysis of, for example, transaction, account, or customer interaction data. It can provide an empirical, objective, and consistent method of evaluating that body of data, and distilling meaning from it that can guide key business decisions.

Predictive models are often called *behavioral models* because they may be used to predict the future behavior of a customer with respect to, for example, their likelihood to become delinquent in repaying loans or to maintain interest-bearing balances in their accounts. By enabling companies to instantly differentiate between desirable, less desirable, and undesirable customers—and, more to the point, to assign different marketing treatments to different customer segments, as well as individual customers, based on their propensity to behave in a certain manner—predictive models allow companies to control the level of risk they are willing to assume and take action to increase profitability.

Predictive models can express interrelated relationships between dozens, hundreds, and even thousands of pieces of data as a single number, a *value score*. This score indicates the likelihood of a certain behavior or event occurring in the future. For instance, a predictive model built to analyze credit risk will produce scores that show which people are most likely to make credit payments on time. Higher scores typically indicate more favorable behavior.

For some people, predictive analytics may simply bring to mind images of an inquisitive child asking yes-or-no questions of a Magic 8 Ball. A round, plastic object with a window that features a decidedly unimpressive interface by today's standards, the toy has delighted children for more than a half century with its promise of being able to "reach into the future to find the answers to your questions." And while those answers often turn out to be highly enigmatic—for example, "It depends" and "Ask me later"—so, too, to be fair, are the answers that are occasionally produced by far more sophisticated techniques for seeing into the future.

Of course, predictive modeling is hardly a new phenomenon. It has long been practiced in the form of statistical forecasting. And what are statistics but the processes by which people should change their expectations or behaviors after having experienced the world? Here's a simple example: *Based on historical climate patterns, September-to-December rainfall in Entebbe was above average 4 out of 10 times during the 10 strongest El Niño events.* And here's the expectation, based on that experience: *Should another strong El Niño event occur, there's a 40 percent chance that September-to-December rainfall in Entebbe will be above average.* Experiences may be natural occurrences—as is the case with El Niño—or designed, otherwise known as experiments. Statistics tell people what actions should be taken so as to optimize a specific process according to some sensible set of criteria. Predictive models codify that optimization.

Indeed, the evolution of predictive modeling in many ways mirrors the shift from marketing automation to marketing optimization. In this context, optimization means being able to analyze large quantities of data, examine numerous combinations of variables, uncover previously hidden relationships—and, ultimately, come to understand and predict customer behavior at a granular level. And the real magic is that it can all happen in the blink of an eye.

Next-generation analytics is made possible by a new breed of data mining applications that leverage faster processing speeds and more complex algorithms to perform three key functions. The first function relates to the automated discovery of patterns that were previously unknown or thought to be inconsequential. The second function relates to "forensic analysis," used primarily by quality assurance and credit card fraud systems. The third function, which is the most relevant in the context of the current discussion, relates to the automated prediction of trends and behaviors. It is the basis for any customer retention program that seeks to segment a customer base in an effort to determine the most profitable category of customer, and predict the ability to retain and leverage that customer relationship through a targeted marketing program.

USING PREDICTIVE MODELING

A rich customer database is critical—knowing whom a company's customers are, what they buy, their likes and dislikes, and so on. However, unless a company uses this information to predict what consumers will do in the future, such a database is of little value. The key to doing so is in predictive modeling. Predictive models transform businesses from being experimental and opportunistic to deliberately and effectively deploying their marketing dollars toward opportunities with reliably predictable outcomes. In precision marketing, predictive modeling occurs in three primary areas:

1. Segmentation
2. Campaign experimentation
3. Call center optimization

Segmentation. Segmentation is not a cross-tab report, nor is it clustering by demographics. Instead, segmentation models account for the complex interactions among many variables, such as: purchasing data, attitudinal information, demographics, propensity to respond, and so on. Statistical modeling uses a variety of data-mining techniques to identify segments of people who share similar behaviors. Understanding these segments allows companies to identify the profiles of highly lucrative customers and then test various marketing campaigns on them.

Campaign Experimentation. Sending a 15 percent discount coupon to a consumer who buys only that company's product loses money—that consumer is unlikely to buy a competing product, so that coupon just loses the company 15 percent of the product's sale price. Sending a 15 percent discount to a brand-switcher, on the other hand, makes more sense. Predictive modeling helps companies determine which consumers are brand-switchers and then individualize promotions, bundling, and pricing strategies to drive the revenue growth among them. Similarly, marketing campaign experiments can determine which consumers account for most of a company's business and which never respond to promotions. Predictive models that identify the "best" and "worst" consumers help companies stop wasting dollars on "worst" consumers and will drive millions of dollars worth of marketing budget savings.

Contact Center Optimization. Experimentation and predictive modeling have also been used very successfully in call centers to increase cross-sell/up-sell revenue, increase collections, and reduce customer attrition. Here's a brief example. A major credit card company has one million accounts a year that go delinquent, representing $1 billion of debt, about half of which is ultimately collected. A study was launched to determine how modifications of the standard first-call collections script could impact the collections' efficacy. Moving to the best single call script (the right message) resulted in an 11 percent increase in collections. Dynamically selecting the best script out of four different options (the right message to the right person) resulted in another two percent increase in collections. Spread across $500 million in annual collections, this represents an impact on the company's profits of more than $50 million annually.

BLUEPRINTING THE IDEAL CUSTOMER

Predicting customer behavior requires the use of advanced modeling and scoring capabilities. Modeling refers to the analysis of customer profile information to uncover the most relevant characteristics of a given customer segment. The process works like this:

Discover.   Look at your existing customer base to identify cross-sell and up-sell opportunities. Use a simple scoring system to generate a roster of your most attractive customers.

Map and Check.   Next, map that roster against external databases of prospective customers. How well do the two lists correlate? Poor correlation portends a gloomy outcome.

Segment by Value.   Construct relevant market segments, organized along value drivers like churn, migration patterns, and so forth. These drivers will vary depending on your industry. For the wireless industry, churn might be the best metric, since the average annual churn is widely reported as 30 percent. Given an industry that loses almost one-third of its customers a year, and where the acquisition cost is as high as $400 per customer, improving retention, even if only slightly, will create extraordinary value. In the consumer packaged goods space, however, where attrition can be much lower, it might be more helpful to evaluate a customer's likelihood to migrate to a premium-priced product.

Anticipate.   Look at the customers in each segment—those who are leaving, migrating, and so forth—and try to find others who show similar characteristics and traits, who might be moving into these segments in the near future. Which customers might be at risk three or four months down the road? Which represent real opportunities now? Having identified these risks and opportunities, the company can then take pre-emptive actions to diminish the likelihood of defection and to increase the possibility of up-sell.

What does success look like when all the pieces are in place? It varies. For example, an insurance company might want to know: "What are the common attributes of customers who purchase life insurance?" Common attributes ascertained from a statistically valid sample pool would indicate the model of customer most likely to purchase life insurance in the future. Having identified these attributes across any number of geodemographic, psychographic, and situational dimensions, the company could then score customers based on the extent to which their profile information corresponds with the model of, in this case, "the life insurance buyer." Customers who fall into the category of Potential Profit Generators can then be targeted with customized offerings based on the overall design of the marketing campaign. Customers with higher value scores might be sent a promotion of one kind, while those with lower scores might be sent a promotion of a different kind.

Typically, a customer segmentation profile for a company's up-sell campaign is based solely on transaction data, which, in reality, represents just one narrow measure that a company might use to score customer value. The scores are tied to the recency, frequency, and monetary value (RFM) of transactions. In this example, the RFM variables might be used to identify those customers who are most likely to respond to a particular up-sell campaign. But, as we previously noted, transactional data reflects only the *current value* of a customer to the company. To get a better handle on a customer's worth in the long run, and to be able to allocate resources accordingly, companies also need to factor *lifetime value* considerations into the equation.

That said, when it comes to using value scores to rank and rate customers, RFM variables are certainly a good place to start. To determine which customers are its biggest profit generators, First Union, the nation's sixth-largest bank, employs software to analyze a CRR that contains 27 terabytes of transaction and other data on 16 million customers. Or consider Canada's largest financial services institution, the Bank of Montreal (BMO), with U.S. $155 billion in assets. In 2002, BMO resolved to destroy its isolated data silos, allowing the customer information to flow across the entire company. It also resolved to score customer profitability in real time, using a tool that segments and ranks customers according to such criteria as their propensity to buy, their preference for buying specific products, and even their likelihood of switching to a competitor. By analyzing information from 18 million accounts across 32 different business lines, the scoring tool enables BMO to build highly refined models to predict which customers would be interested in buying any number of different financial products the bank offers, and to then reach out to them in a highly targeted manner.

It's not surprising that the correlation between predictive ability and increased profitability is most striking in the financial services industry. Generally speaking, the industry is far ahead of the customer analytics curve relative to other market sectors. As our examples suggest, banks are especially keen to analyze customer data in their quest to discern the common attributes among "perfect customers," which might simply translate into those customers who carry a significant balance on their credit cards but who also pay regularly. Thus a bank may decide to eliminate these customers' annual fee and offer them other attractive, profitable programs, all the while seeking new customers who fit the perfect customer profile.

Recently, Chase Manhattan Bank conducted an exercise to determine whether those customers who complain about minimum checking balances are actually profitable—or, conversely, whether they are money-losing propositions. Should the bank simply dispose of the customers if the cost to serve them exceeds the value derived from them, by allowing them to defect to a competitor that offers lower minimum balances? The answer may not be as simple as it at first seems. For example, companies may wish to factor in *network effects*—the fact that happy customers tend to bring in other customers, significantly growing the customer base while reducing customer acquisition costs.

Also, as we have said, companies must avoid valuing customers based solely on their present value. The fact of the matter is that today's most profitable customers might *not* be a company's best bet. In fact, a company's best bet might be today's *least* profitable customers. Treating customers in a certain way based on present value rather than option value considerations represents a deeply flawed segmentation logic. Instead, companies should strive to collect and analyze customer data that would help determine which customers at, say, the "bronze level" ought to be escalated to, say, the "gold level," based on their future value *potential*. Again, projecting that potential means using predictive modeling techniques to anticipate whether a customer, based on various profile indicators, is likely to *later*—whether in five months or in five years—qualify for that higher level of service. In which case, it may very well make sense to subsidize the higher cost of serving that customer in the short term.

So, in order to maximize the value of its customer base, a company needs to take two courses of action, on a continuous basis. The first course of action is to identify those customers who are as close as possible to spending their potential on the company's products and services, and then matching the right level of sales and service to maintain or further strengthen those relationships. This is Customer Relationship Management 101. The second, more challenging, course of action is to identify those customers who are currently only moderately profitable but who have the potential to be more profitable in the future, and to then act accordingly. Making calculations on the probability of events happening or not happening—or, in this case, on customers becoming profitable or not profitable—requires that companies go full throttle on their predictive modeling capabilities. Again, these models can paint a much clearer picture of which customers to invest in, versus the traditional approach of blindly investing in only today's most profitable customers. After all, as any restaurant-goer knows, good restaurants can go bad, and bad restaurants can go out of business. The same can be said of customers.

Here's a related question to ponder: If you're a financial services company armed with the profile information of millions of customers, should you limit the scope of your activities to financial services? Faced with increasing amounts of "information exhaust"—customer and transactional records that at one time seemed worthless but which, upon further reflection, could serve as the basis for deeper analysis—a number of banks have come to realize that their businesses are not just finance-related, but also information-related. Increasingly, they are coming to view financial services as the aperture through which to market additional products and services, from magazine subscriptions to mobile phones.

By inventorying all of their customer data, and breaking it down into its elemental components, companies across all types of industries may well discover some hidden gems. Can data be deployed in creative ways to launch new offerings, propelling the business tangentially into adjacent opportunity arenas? Can it serve as a vector for growth, a springboard that could potentially catapult the company to the next level of valuation? Ask H&R Block. A few years ago, the company leveraged its customer data to grow its business beyond tax-preparation services, to include mortgage, retirement planning, and investment services. Clearly, CEO Mark Ernst had access to a Magic 8 Ball! In 2002, in the midst of a recession, the company reported a 55 percent increase in net earnings over the previous year, with revenues totaling $3.3 billion. Revenues reached $3.78 billion the following year, with earnings expected to grow by 18 percent in 2004, largely on the strength of the company's mortgage operations. For H&R Block, leveraging customer data turned out to be a very smart move, indeed.

This chapter opened with a quote by Ken Kesey, the celebrated author of *One Flew over the Cuckoo's Nest*. He remarked: "You can count the number of seeds in an apple, but you can't count the number of apples in a seed." Kesey's words resonate strongly in the context of customer data analytics. In particular, his words can be interpreted to mean that a company can determine the *present value* of its customer base, but not the *future value* of an individual customer. This was true enough in the past. Today, however, the ability to "count the number of apples in a seed" is fast becoming a reality. So, too, is it now possible to target those "seeds," or customers, that will eventually bear the most fruit.

4
PRECISION MARKETING IN THE AGE OF GAIA

The entire range of living matter on Earth from whales to viruses and from oaks to algae could be regarded as constituting a single living entity capable of maintaining the Earth's atmosphere to suit its overall needs and endowed with faculties and powers far beyond those of its constituent parts.

—James Lovelock[1]

Working out of his office at the Jet Propulsion Laboratory in Pasadena, California, in the mid-1960s, a British geochemist by the name of James Lovelock experienced a profound revelation. It came to him as an unexpected mental leap, an "Aha!" of such proportions that it would guide his intellectual journey for decades to come, into the next century.

When lightning struck, Lovelock was deep in the throes of designing scientific instruments for NASA's Mars *Viking* probes. The purpose of the assignment was to detect the presence of life on Mars.

In going about the task, Lovelock operated under the assumption that the most fundamental characteristic of all life is not just the need to consume energy and discard waste, but the use of the planet's atmosphere as a medium for this cyclic exchange. If there were life on Mars, he reasoned, then it would leave a chemical signature on the planet's atmosphere. Finding no evidence of such a signature, Lovelock concluded that the Martian atmosphere is *not* in "dynamic equilibrium" with the planet's surface.

At the same time, Lovelock found that Earth's atmosphere *is* in dynamic equilibrium with *its* surface; moreover, living organisms as well as inorganic materials—the air, oceans, and rocks—keep it that way. Together, these different components make the environment suitable for life itself. This notion that Earth sits at the core of a unified, cooperating, and living system challenged just about everyone's thinking. The theory was named *the Gaia hypothesis*, after the Greek goddess of Earth.

According to Lovelock, Earth survives in a hostile environment—space—because of the close relationships among the biosphere, atmosphere, hydrosphere, and geosphere. Each of these components acts in concert with the other components to ensure the ongoing survival of the planet. By the same token, we submit that a company survives in a hostile environment—the marketplace—because of the close relationships among suppliers, partners, employees, and customers. Each of these components acts in concert with the other components to ensure the ongoing survival of the *extended business network*.[2]

Substitute a few words and suddenly Lovelock's definition of Gaia becomes the perfect lens through which to view the myriad forces collectively reshaping the world of business. These forces have been at work for more than two decades, driven by two interrelated phenomena: the digitization of information and the networking of companies.

Recently, the changes wrought by these forces have accelerated, due to the proliferation of Internet-based systems, standards, and software applications that give companies new ways to buy, make, and sell—*collaboratively*. Collaborative planning. Collaborative design. Collaborative engineering. Collaborative sourcing. Collaborative manufacturing. Collaborative distribution. Collaborative learning. Collaborative selling. Collaborative marketing. To be sure, collaborative tools are the saving grace of the e-business revolution. They're the glistening pearls that remained behind after that tumultuous ocean of hype evaporated back into the blue sky. And like all precious gems, their value endures.

Going forward, companies will continue to harness the power of network technology to improve their operational capabilities—which, to a large degree, means extending their core operations beyond the conventional boundaries of the organization. The Internet gave rise to countless new companies, including a few whose business models did, in fact, revolutionize entire industries. But there's no mistaking its greater impact: *to enable businesses to better manage their interactions with key stakeholders.* Today, thanks to end-to-end process visibility, an internal project team can work hand-in-hand with an external project team, interacting in real time, with access to the same view of the data, as if all were employees of the same company under the same roof.

Such a state of collaboration redefines the very concept of *outsourcing*. After all, outsourcing assumes that a rigid boundary exists between the inside and outside of a company. But when a company's partners become seamlessly connected in the manner described, they can simply become an extension of an integrated system. To quote Lovelock, they can become a part of "a single living entity."

THE RISE OF BUSINESS PROCESS OUTSOURCING (BPO)

The word *system* comes from the Greek word *synhistanai*, meaning *a complex whole put together*. As our metaphorical use of the Gaia hypothesis suggests, an extended business network is exactly that: a whole system. It's a collection of elements where the performance of the whole is affected by each of its parts. The interconnectedness of the different companies that contribute to the network, and their propensity to work together to improve the system as a whole, reflect a key insight of the Gaia hypothesis. In particular, it suggests that companies compete less on the basis of isolated resources and capabilities, and more on the *totality* of the network's resources and capabilities. Today this seismic shift is being further intensified by the growth of *business process outsourcing (BPO)*.

As the term suggests, BPO involves the contracting out of various business functions to outside providers. And today, practically every large company outsources some portion of its major business processes. The reasons are easy to understand. BPO can allow a company to concentrate its resources on the aspects of its business that are unique to its existence while leveraging the scale and capabilities of other companies that have more advanced capabilities and specialized expertise already in place. In this way, BPO further narrows the scope of what a company does in-house while broadening the scope of what it orchestrates through its network of partners. The movement is fueled by the promise of lower deployment costs, reduced complexity, increased speed of deployment, greater agility, and reduced operating risks.

Of course, outsourcing has been a mainstay of business strategy for decades, if not centuries—arguably, ever since a consortium of fifteenth century Venetian monks got the bright idea to "outsource" the reproduction of their sacred books to merchant printers. (It sure beat copying the text by hand themselves.) The Great Depression kicked off the modern era of outsourcing, with outside vendors producing component parts or even assembling and delivering the final product. Outsourced manufacturing has since become a basic tenet of modern business. It underlies the production of all types of consumer goods, from cars and sneakers to designer clothes and handheld computers. Case in point: Palm products are made by Flextronics, a leader in electronics contract manufacturing; meanwhile, to compete with Palm in the PDA market, Dell Computer placed big bets on its own Axim X5, which is made by Wistron, a Taiwanese manufacturer.

Generally speaking, it might be said that BPO involves *bits*, not *atoms*. It's less about using outside vendors to pour the plastic molding and count the metal fittings, and more about using them to process, convert, and analyze data, and to facilitate information flow for practically any back-office or front-office function—better, cheaper, and faster. Also with BPO, the role of the outside vendor should transcend *technical responsibility*. While, clearly, the need to assume some degree of technical responsibility was a requirement of even the earliest IT outsourcing initiatives, in the 1980s, companies now expect something more. That something more takes the form of *process expertise.*

BPO is commonly described as the transfer of nonrevenue-generating activities to third parties that have specialized resources already in place to perform the same activities more efficiently. No doubt, it's important to do things more efficiently. But these partners also need to create *strategic value*, by leveraging technologies and expertise in highly innovative ways to reengineer—and, possibly, even reinvent—processes altogether. This perspective reflects the fundamental difference between efficiency and effectiveness that we touch on in Chapter 1.

The shift in emphasis from technical responsibility to process expertise is mirrored in the fact that companies previously sought to outsource only those processes that did *not* directly contribute to shareholder value. HR benefits management, payroll processing, procurement, content management, and internal auditing are just a few examples. Importantly, companies today have also taken to outsourcing processes that *do* directly contribute to shareholder value—most notably, the customer communication process.

Customer call center operations, in particular, represent an enormous growth sector in the BPO arena, due to the substantial cost savings that companies can stand to realize. Today much of that growth is taking place offshore, as plunging communication costs and technical advances around telecommunications infrastructures make it possible to tap skilled but low-cost work forces in countries such as India and the Philippines, where the quality of customer service can equal—or even exceed—that of local outsourced call centers. In India alone, BPO revenues—mainly from call center operations—are forecast to grow from $2 billion in 2003 to $21 billion in 2008.

OUTSOURCING PIECES OF THE PRECISION MARKETING CYCLE

Practically every company today is asking the same question: "How do we improve the productivity and effectiveness of our marketing process and programs?" As we make clear in previous chapters, at least part of the answer resides in precision marketing. In addition, for many companies, at least part of the answer lies beyond the four walls of the organization. Put them together—*precision marketing on an outsourced basis*—and some hall-pacing marketing executives may finally get a good night's sleep.

What we mean by precision marketing on an outsourced basis is that some—if not all—of the technology components that comprise the customer-facing application suite (CFAS), which we described in the previous chapter, and that ultimately brings precision marketing programs to life, can now be enabled through external partners. Again, in addition to the customer relationship repository, these components include the channel manager, the campaign manager, and the analytics manager.

For many large companies, the ability to rent access to a component-based CFAS architecture on a subscription basis presents a tremendous array of advantages over the alternative of installing, operating, and maintaining each of the individual components using the company's own internal IT and marketing resources. By partnering with a best-of-breed service provider, companies can decide which marketing applications and services they want to subscribe to, and add/delete/modify these individual offerings from a unified CFAS framework. Again, the applications encompass the key functions that drive customer attraction, retention, and leverage. They should work together as seamlessly as possible—all the while allowing companies to evolve their marketing architectures as their needs change without having to tear apart their own IT systems, and without fear of becoming entrapped in costly upgrades or inferior vendor choices. Think of it as marketing optimization, without all the mess!

In addition to the software, there's the "peopleware" side of the equation to consider. The right human expertise can make any business process run smoother, of course, but it becomes an especially important consideration in the context of analytics management, given the limitations of any software application to meaningfully interpret data patterns, conduct the right sets of experiments, and work with the rest of the marketing organization to assign the optimal treatment to each customer segment. The need to create actionable intelligence from massive amounts of customer data on an ongoing basis can pose a considerable challenge for companies that may have suitable technology systems in place but still lack the necessary experience and expertise. Hence the call for a highly trained team of statisticians, market research analysts, and behavioral scientists with a deep understanding of the customer analytics discipline as it applies to precision marketing, preferably within a specific industry context.

We know firsthand, based on our own client work, that the economic value of "real analytics" over simple cross-tabulations can be stunning. We also know that working at a high level of sophistication requires the integration of diverse skill sets and operational excellence. Gathering all of the right analytical resources in one place also requires a scale operation to be economically feasible, which is one strong argument for analytics outsourcing. In addition, moving the analytics function to the jurisdiction of an external partner can provide the internal marketing organization with much-needed objectivity. Unbiased opinion can diffuse spats, as marketers tussle over the best way to allocate their limited dollars.

In terms of mitigating the risk factors, we're big proponents of a benefits-based pricing model that ties service fees to performance outcomes. By having a tailored business relationship based on shared risks and shared rewards, the vendor's fortunes become contingent on the actual benefits it delivers, tracked using quantifiable success metrics. It's easily done, given the strong link between precision marketing implementation and Marketing ROI. Incremental sales lifts translate into incremental service fees. Period. Today we're seeing the "gain sharing" trend ripple across the entire sea of professional services—including the traditional, full-service ad agencies, where the compensation structure continues to undergo significant change. In recent years, agency work has tended to shift from commission-based to fixed fee, time, and materials-based—that is, X deliverables for Y hours plus Z markup. "Now, everything's on the table," laments one agency executive. "The economics are shifting to the point that we're just happy to cover our costs and then share in any potential upside. We'll co-invest with our clients in an idea." Problem is, the link between mass marketing and Marketing ROI is circuitous, as we've shown, making the payment scheme a challenge.

Many executives love the idea of outsourcing the optimization of their customer data to a firm that excels at doing exactly that. For others, however, the idea can feel like a giant leap of faith. After all, they reason, that data is a cornerstone of their company's competitive strength, a main engine of value creation. They wonder: "Can we really entrust an external vendor to manage part or all of our customer-facing functions?" In reality, *nobody* should know what a company's marketing strategy ought to be better than its own internal marketing organization. (We get to the other trust issues a bit later.)

In our view, the demarcation is clear. Companies are wise to keep the underlying business logic skills, resource allocation decisions, and overall marketing objectives in-house. But as the objectives become clear, and the marketing organization firms up the exact nature of its strategy and tactics, the actual implementation can be outsourced to a service provider (or multiple vendors) that can more effectively, quickly, and cheaply deliver against those objectives. When it comes to overall marketing strategy, therefore, companies would be wise to insource the thinking and outsource the implementation.

Outsourcing the implementation gives marketers, and the internal IT organizations that support them, the freedom to turn their attention to issues of greater strategic importance than the tedium of software upgrades, systems integration, and network maintenance. Moreover, as we've suggested, marketing executives should not have to worry about placing bets on expensive technology platforms at a time when the winners and losers are all but obvious. Instead, they should focus on garnering strategic insights from their customer data and pushing the envelope on their marketing programs, to maximize the value of that data.

The idea of precision marketing isn't exactly new to the world, as we've said—and neither, for that matter, is the idea of marketing outsourcing. Ever since 1843, when the first advertising agency hung its shingle in Philadelphia, companies have relied on third parties to supplement or even assume full ownership of their various marketing functions. As shown in Figure 4.1, these functions have long included all forms of advertising and promotion, public relations, market research, marketing communications, and customer support. Marketing mix analytics began to gather steam in the 1990s, along with the development and management of Internet-based customer touch points. In this context, precision marketing simply represents the next step on the staircase.

FROM DATA INTEGRATION TO *EXPERIENCE* INTEGRATION

In an era of business process outsourcing, a company's inside and outside boundaries gradually disappear. From a customer perspective, it can be hard to know where one company ends and another one begins. The danger lies in the fact that, with every company becoming part of a broader solution that involves a greater number of handoffs, customer satisfaction is sure to suffer whenever the baton gets dropped. Consequently, as customer satisfaction comes to depend on every partner delivering incremental value that accumulates into a positive, end-

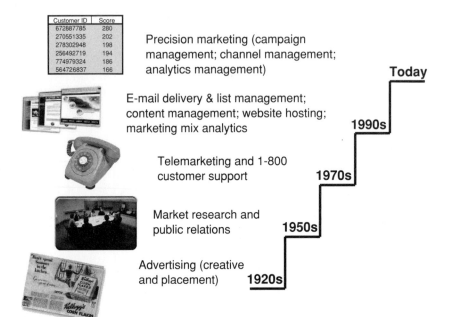

FIGURE 4.1   The Evolution of Marketing Outsourcing

to-end customer experience, a company's overall performance can easily become a reflection of that of its partners.

Customer experience is a key consideration as companies build out their constellation of partnerships—since, again, it involves the *totality* of the customer's interactions with the company. Most companies no longer have exclusive ownership over customer interactions. When a customer subscribes to a phone or cable service, for example, or buys a car or an airline ticket, there may be multiple points of interaction, each one facilitated by a different company wearing the hat of the same company.

"It can take incredible acrobatics to make the customer experience come together in a meaningful way," notes one executive. "Yet as you look to expand your market opportunity with the customer, it becomes important to not only use outsourced vendors but also to offer outsourced products." Take the case of SBC Communications, whose outsourced products include satellite TV and wireless phone service. The new offerings were integrated into SBC's portfolio as part of an overall effort to maximize the synergies between SBC and Cingular, the nation's second largest wireless carrier, in which SBC owns a 60 percent stake. In 2003, the two companies also initiated joint sales, marketing, and planning activities. While providing customers with a unified resource for wireless services makes a lot of sense, the challenge lies in creating a positive customer experience as the two companies work to package the different products and services together.

In integrating customer-facing processes across all of the different players—from online brokers and resellers to e-mail service providers and overseas call centers—the objective is to deliver a seamless experience, so that customers can see "a single face" and hear "a single voice" when they interact with the company. More importantly, the objective is to deliver a *positive* experience.

Consider Amazon's multiyear agreement with Circuit City, which gives customers who order electronic goods from Amazon the option of picking up those goods in any one of 600 Circuit City store locations. Amazon processes the transaction while Circuit City handles order fulfillment and product-related customer service. A perfect match. But what if an Amazon customer were to have a disappointing experience with Circuit City? The company has no record of that customer's online transaction, for example. To some extent, the experience would also reflect poorly on Amazon. (Fortunately, to our knowledge, this has never been the case.)

Shortcomings on the part of a partner can cause a company to not only miss out on new revenue opportunities but also damage its existing revenue streams. It's an important fact to bear in mind in the context of precision marketing. Imagine a scenario in which e-mail messages sent on behalf of PepsiCo by Yahoo! Direct, a Pepsi e-mail service provider, were to continue unabated, despite repeated requests by irritated recipients to unsubscribe from future updates. Such a blunder might eventually push even the most ardent Pepsi drinker toward the Coke camp. Or imagine a scenario in which a Best Buy customer picks up the phone to inquire about a store promotion, only to have an unpleasant encounter with the CSR—who, in reality, is an employee not of Best Buy but of eTelecare, the outsourced call center that provides Best Buy's inbound voice services. Such an incident could potentially tarnish the retailer's reputation in the eyes of that particular customer. Fortunately, as far as we know, Pepsi couldn't be happier with Yahoo! Direct, and Best Buy and eTelecare remain best friends.

CAPTURING AND USING CUSTOMER KNOWLEDGE ACROSS THE EXTENDED BUSINESS NETWORK

There's an old joke about a drunk who has lost his house keys. He is on his knees under a street lamp when a passerby offers to help him in the search. But after some time with no success, the passerby asks the drunk, "Where did you lose your keys?" The drunk replies, "Outside my front door." "Then why are we looking for them out here under the street lamp?" asks the passerby. "Because," replies the drunk, "there is more light here."

Companies that fail to capture customer transaction and interaction data in a consistent way across their customer-facing channels can begin to resemble the drunk who has lost his house keys. Consider the fact that most consumer packaged goods companies make their strategic marketing decisions based solely on grocery store transaction data, even though they may also do a substantial amount of business in the food services realm outside of retail. In other words, these CPG companies may shine a

1,000-watt spotlight on grocery store chains while allowing other reseller channels to operate in complete darkness. Needless to say, companies that capture customer data from some channels and not others tend to run into problems when it comes to making smart marketing decisions.

Skewed data collection can prevent marketers from creating 360-degree views of customer behavior, making it difficult to build predictive models. Moreover, it can make it impossible to determine the profitability of different customer segments. After all, as a first order of business, analyzing customer segment profitability requires that information across all communication and sales channels, including those channels that operate under the jurisdiction of partner companies, be collected and then integrated into a centralized repository. The challenge, aside from the common hurdles related to data integration, is that not all partners are hired guns and not all companies that collaborate are necessarily in close cahoots—or, for that matter, philosophically aligned in terms of a common cause. Fact is, some players within the extended business network may be *unwilling* to share the customer information that they collect.

Such a possibility brings us to the overly hyped and ultimately presumptuous question: Who owns the customer? The answer, of course, is *nobody*. Yet the real question—Who controls access to the customer data?—sits at the very heart of precision marketing. The question has become highly contentious in many extended business networks where multiple stakeholders touch the customer at various stages.

Consider a network that centers on the production, sales, and distribution of automobiles. It used to be that cars were built by automakers and customer relationships were managed by dealerships, and never the twain met. Today, however, several different players have the ability to collect and manipulate large amounts of demographic, financial, behavioral, and other types of consumer data that may offer insights into the kinds of vehicles that a customer may want to buy, either now or at some point down the road. Yet some dealers refuse to share customer data with automakers, fearing that the automakers might, in turn, share it with other dealers that compete for the same customers, or perhaps even use it to establish factory-direct sales. At the same time, automakers argue they need data garnered at the dealerships so they can learn more about customer preferences, and therefore, what vehicles to build for the marketplace. Gaining access to the data allows automakers to not only focus their efforts on satisfying the needs of current customers but, potentially, to better understand their "genetic makeup" so as to be able to market to others just like them. Again, we refer to this process as *blueprinting the ideal customer*.

Some evidence suggests that dealers and automakers are beginning to warm up to a more collaborative model in terms of sharing customer information. Toyota, for example, recently launched a pilot program with five Toyota and six Lexus dealers to test the waters on how customer data might be shared to everyone's advantage. Toyota reportedly believes that relationship building starts with the dealer, and views itself as playing a supporting role in the marketplace. The pilot program has dealers sending their customer data to Toyota's analytics team, which then reciprocates with actionable reports designed to help the dealers enhance customer service and increase customer retention.

Of course, at the same time that companies need to collect customer data from all customer interaction points and store it in the customer relationship repository, companies also need to make customer information accessible at all customer interaction points. Nordstrom makes its individual customer profiles available to its clerks at the point of sale, allowing them to tell the best in-store shoppers—customers who spend $2,000 more per year than other shoppers—about new merchandise arrivals and store events. By the same token, companies need to make the same kinds of information available to their customer-facing partners. For example, CSRs located in customer call centers in Manila and

Bangladore need to see the customer information on their screens, along with automated matchups—if only in the form of "first offers" and "back-down offers," based on the caller's segmentation profile—in order to be able to cross-sell and up-sell as well as those Nordstrom clerks located in the Chicago suburbs.

CREATING A "RELATIONSHIP MIND SET"

Today, a company's ability to capture profits from its activities stems not from the ownership of plants, equipment, and inventory but from the orchestration of relationships. For this reason, companies need to adopt a "relationship mind set," a term recently trumpeted by Ford Motor Company in its campaign to boost shareholder confidence in the face of sagging shareholder value.

A relationship mind set means broadening the view to include not only customers, but also partners, suppliers, and even the company's own employees in the value equation. Raytheon Company, the $17 billion defense, government, and commercial electronics contractor, articulates this broader view on its website: "Each of our successes reflects the united efforts of a strong, diverse network of employees, suppliers, and partner companies."

Broadening the view means playing a whole new ballgame—one in which the players in the outfield and those in the infield join as a single, integrated superplayer. To some extent, it also means inventing a new scoreboard, given the limitations of our 500-year-old accounting system to adequately track the corporate equivalents of runs batted in and cumulative performance.

After all, if relationships matter so much—if, indeed, we're to subscribe to the tagline for Chase, the $755 billion global financial services institution, that *the right relationship is everything*—then shouldn't relationships show up as assets on a company's balance sheet? If only we could ask Luca Pacioli.

Luca Pacioli was one of those fifteenth century Venetian monks who pioneered the concept of outsourcing. He is also widely credited as the first person to document the principles of double-entry bookkeeping, and is even thought by some historians to have actually invented it. If that is true, Pacioli can hardly be faulted for thinking only in terms of a scale for weighing physical assets. After all, the basic economic resources of fifteenth century Italy were materials, labor, and capital. These same resources served as the basis for wealth creation for centuries to come, until the end of the industrial age.

Fast forward half a millennium. Nowadays, resources can be divided into four broad categories: (1) resources that exist in physical form, also known as *structural capital*; (2) resources that exist as cash and cash equivalents, also known as *financial capital*; (3) resources that reside in people, also known as *intellectual capital*; and, lastly, (4) resources that take the form of relationships, also known as *relationship capital*.

Over the past couple of decades, the most valuable resources of a typical company have shifted from structural capital to intellectual and relationship capital. The shift has led to a mismatch between the accounting rules by which companies must abide and the market capitalizations that Wall Street assigns to them. For investors, the mismatch has become problematic.

The problem is that generally accepted accounting principles (GAAP) insist on treating physical resources such as smoke-billowing factories and inventory-filled warehouses as assets while treating intangible assets, including investments in customer service and partner management, as expenses. No matter that the latter may create far more economic value than the former. Perhaps the reason has to do with the financial reports' originally intended audience: the bankers, who naturally preferred to lend money against resources that could be repossessed, if necessary. Bankers would be hard-pressed to repossess a relationship! In any case, regulatory agencies continue to pay scant attention to the implications of measuring anything other than physical assets, thereby entrapping investors in a bygone era of financial reporting.

In reality, invisible beans are hard to count. The Financial Accounting Standards Board and The American Institute of Certified Public Accountants would be hard-pressed to institute a set of accounting practices for valuing intangible assets. What would they look like? How could a company place a monetary value on a trusted partnership? What metrics might be used to impute this value? Access to new markets? Reduced marketing and sales expenses? Such metrics are difficult to quantify, and in most cases could be applied only in a relative manner, by weighing the performance of one partner against that of another. Sure, a reliable network of partners eliminates the search and coordination costs associated with the negotiation of contracts, while mitigating the risk of partner misconduct or nonperformance. Yet there's no way to translate such benefits into the language of money.

By the same token, how could a company place a monetary value on the strength of its customer relationships? What about imputing a value for customer satisfaction—which, after all, drives customer loyalty and brand equity? The fact that companies commonly trade at several times book value is, at its core, a function of the level of perceived customer satisfaction, which—along with various external factors—naturally informs investors' expectations about future profitability. Clearly, a decline in customer satisfaction would foretell an erosion of future profitability, if only investors had this type of information at their disposal.

Many people believe that investors would have a better understanding of the relationship between a company's current condition and its future capacity to create wealth if accounting could incorporate customer satisfaction as an asset on the balance sheet. One group even launched an economic indicator of customer evaluations of the quality of products and services, called the American Customer Satisfaction Index.* The Index is a step in the right direction. Yet it's still a far cry from a standard model of company valuation that incorporates the strength of customer relationships.

---

*The American Customer Satisfaction Index was launched in 1994 by The University of Michigan Business School, the American Society for Quality, and the consulting firm CFI Group.

USING TRUST TO MAINTAIN
"DYNAMIC EQUILIBRIUM"

In the world of intangible assets, definitions collide, boundaries blur, and instability prevails. To be sure, intangible assets can be capricious and demand no small amount of attention. *Ignore them*, one might say, only half jokingly, *and they'll go away*. Partner relationships are especially likely to take missteps that can put them on the slippery slope to failure. In the blink of an eye, it seems, good partnerships can go bad, and bad partnerships can wreak irreparable damage.

Nowhere is this lesson taught to greater effect than in the infamous breakdown of one of the most enduring partnerships in American industry: Ford, the second largest automaker, and Firestone, its leading supplier of tires for more than 95 years. The breakdown, marked by the production of defective tires thought to be responsible for up to 200 deaths, culminated in numerous lawsuits, a Congressional investigation, and a recall that contributed heavily toward Ford's combined total of $6.4 billion in losses in 2001 and 2002. That's not to mention Firestone's forfeiture of $300 million in annual sales to Ford—an enormous price in itself to have to pay.

In hindsight, the tragedy can be seen as a cautionary tale about what can happen when shareholder expectations take precedence over the best interests of suppliers, employees, and customers. The story is well known: Ford, reportedly concerned about missing its quarterly earnings projections, allegedly pressured its suppliers to lower prices to an untenable level. In fact, Ford is said to have demanded a price reduction of up to 5 percent from its suppliers in recent years, making it difficult for them to realize any earnings above their cost of capital. While the apparent result of the pressure on Firestone didn't surface until August 2000, when the press first reported the bad news, any trace of loyalty between the two companies had clearly evaporated long before that date.

Could the Ford/Firestone tragedy have been avoided if only

the two companies had built their relationship on a more solid foundation of trust, sustained it by a greater sense of mutual gain, and facilitated it by a more open flow of information? Perhaps. Evidence suggests that Firestone received warranty data that documented the defective tires early on but declined to share that information with Ford. It was a communications breakdown for which both companies would pay dearly.

"*Partnership* must be more than a word," declares a West African proverb. "It must be a behavior." So, what kind of behavior must companies put into practice in order to create and sustain healthy, functional partnerships—or, for that matter, any type of business relationships? Most people would agree that *mutual respect* is one such precondition. So, too, is a willingness to assume a certain amount of *risk*. The risk that a partner will disregard quality control standards, for example, or drag its feet when it comes time to integrate new systems, resulting in a missed market opportunity. Also important is the need to establish some element of *trust*—which, upon deeper reflection, goes hand-in-hand with risk. After all, what good is trust in an environment devoid of risk? Conversely, in an environment fraught with risk, where the waves of uncertainty buffet us in every direction, trust can be the only safe harbor.

In a world where multiple companies work together to achieve a common purpose in a seamless torrent of interconnected, complementary activities, with each company performing those activities in which it is best suited, trust is fast becoming a requisite facet of modern business. In deploying enterprise applications centered on collaboration, companies need to foster even greater levels of mutual trust. Putting a technology solution into place to automate a company's supply chain, for example, involves more than just software acquisition and systems integration. In addition, it requires that mutual trust be forged with suppliers given the need to share proprietary information on scheduling, production capacities, and cost targets. As a prerequisite to any type of real collaboration—including scenarios that involve sharing, integrating, and enhancing customer data—

there must be a willingness to open the books in both directions. Seldom, however, is this prerequisite easily fulfilled.

Trust is a strange animal in the corporate world. It has no operating manual, and it can't be easily quantified. Its inputs and outputs are highly ambiguous. It can't be codified into a business process or checklist. And like other intangible assets, it appears nowhere on the balance sheet. There's no limit to the tasks formerly performed by human beings that can now be partially, if not completely, automated, from purchasing, manufacturing, and assembly to sorting and distribution. Yet the degree to which one company declares its reliance on the integrity and character of another company, and then acts accordingly, remains judgment based, and subject to the foibles of human error.

Today more than ever, trust is an imperative that underlies the productivity of *all* business relationships, including those with customers, employees, and even service providers that manage core business processes on an outsourced basis. Yet trust is something that must be earned over time. It can't be bought at a Super Wal-Mart. While the tagline for Dreft, a P&G product for well over a century, makes the glib promise of "a clean you can trust," what works for a consumer's relationship with a laundry detergent washes out completely with respect to a manufacturer's relationship with a supplier of raw materials or component parts. Real trust isn't something that can be simply promised, no matter how large the typeface on a pretty pink box.

Trust generally evolves out of a demonstrated commitment to work together collaboratively, solve problems jointly, and share responsibility for any operational problems that arise. Arrangements based solely on financial transactions, without any sort of long-range philosophy that would encourage partners to place a high value on trust are exactly that: arrangements based on transactions. And these breed a different animal altogether.

Again, consider Ford's long, checkered history of trying to maximize its bargaining power. In a way, Ford almost represents the antithesis of a company sensitized to promoting a spirit of positive change through collaboration. For their part, Ford's suppliers often complained of ruthless demands to cut prices, not to mention unfair paybacks for design innovations. But of course all this is water over the dam, or so we're told. In its 2000 Annual Report, Ford explicitly recognizes the importance of its relationships as an unparalleled source of competitive strength, and implicitly resolves to mend its ways in how it cares for these relationships. "Ford Motor Company is building relationships," it declares in the opening passage of that report. "We're connecting with our customers, suppliers, dealers, society, investors, and employees with better ideas and a relationship mindset." A year later, as the company's earnings slumped even further in the wake of an economic downturn that would inflict significant pain across the entire business landscape, William Clay Ford, the newly installed CEO as well as the great-grandson of both Henry Ford and Harvey Firestone, reiterated the belief that a "relationship mindset" held the key to putting the company back on the right track. "You can't rebuild the business if you don't have strong partnerships," he told reporters, in what would become a familiar refrain over the next couple of years.

In contrast to Ford's battlefield of broken relationships, Japanese automakers have long embraced the benefits of collaboration, going to great lengths over the years to invest in key partners and strengthen their strategic relationships. Toyota and Honda, in particular, boast a solid track record of working collaboratively with suppliers in ways that have allowed them to eliminate expensive process steps, develop modular components that can be easily assembled, and exploit the virtues of lean production. As early as two decades ago, Toyota and Honda were producing cars with defect rates on the order of one-third the standard among comparable U.S. models. At the same time, they maintained a cost advantage of nearly 30 percent. While the gap has since narrowed, the attitude of shared risks and shared rewards continues to pay off in spades, if solid revenue growth in an adverse economy and recent strides in capturing U.S. market share are any indication.

The ideology of "work hard, put your trust in us, and we'll

take care of you in the long run" underlies the maintenance of a healthy system. It's a key insight that the Gaia hypothesis captures quite nicely. Just as Gaia is said to be a complex system of interdependent and mutually sustaining parts interacting in dynamic equilibrium, so, too, must a company's strategic relationships maintain a healthy state of equilibrium with respect to the demands and tradeoffs of the other key constituents. If profoundly disturbed from this state due to economic pressures, breaches of trust, or any other reason, the result can be a collapse of the entire system. To maintain a healthy state of equilibrium, companies face the difficult challenge of managing continual change while remaining sensitive to the unique interests of all of the different participants in the joint value proposition.

A WORD ABOUT CONTRACTS

As companies extend their reach through relationships, it becomes important to realize that there are two governance mechanisms that determine how they can work together. The first way is through the use of a contract for a transaction, which is to say: "If we're going to do a one-time deal with you, then let's sign a piece of paper where we spell out the specifics of the deal, and we'll then hold you to that contract."

Yet, by its very nature, no matter how good the intentions, how diligent the review process, and how competent the legal counsel, a contract will always be incomplete, simply because not every possible contingency can be written into a contract. There will always be missing clauses, omitted terms, and misplaced subsections. Still, whenever there exists an element of distrust, a company will spend an inordinate amount of time refining the wording of its contracts and doing everything possible to make them complete.

The other, ultimately more productive way to conduct business is through a relationship. As we've said, relationships evolve out of a series of repeated transactions. A "serious" relationship can greatly reduce the need to spell out all of the specific terms surrounding those transactions. Over time, as the trust builds, a relationship can grow to accommodate a large range of ad hoc and unforeseen requirements, to the point where, for example, a company might tell a supplier, "Okay, send us x number of parts; we don't have the money to pay you today, but we can pay you next month." Allowing for this kind of flexibility captures the very essence of a relationship-oriented world. In this world, the legal counsel on both sides of the table spend far less time redrafting and renegotiating contracts.

Contracts are written to conform to the letter of the law. They are designed to cross every t and dot every i. In a sense, contracts serve as a substitute for trust; the less trust that exists between two parties, the greater the need for a contract that protects both their interests. Relationships, on the other hand, are the fill-in-the-blanks. They roam free from the shackles of legal documentation. Such flexibility is important in a world where changes need to happen both quickly and frequently. Contracts impose rigidity, whereas relationships offer the flexibility to navigate those changes.

"In competitive behavior, someone always loses," observed the mathematician John Nash, as portrayed by Russell Crowe in the 2002 Oscar-winning movie *A Beautiful Mind*. His observation, which strongly echoes the resource-based view of competitive strategy—and also, incidentally, foreshadows his own work on game theory—essentially visualizes competition as a zero-sum game. So, too, does an observation made, however less eloquently, by Ray Kroc, the founder of McDonald's: "This is rat eat rat, dog eat dog," he once remarked. "I'll kill 'em, and I'm going to kill 'em before they kill me."

This perspective leads one to conclude that there can be only two possible outcomes as companies pursue greater profitability and market share: *win or lose*. When growth is slow, one company's gains are matched by another company's losses; and indeed, throughout business history, the pervasive mentality has

179

always been: "My win is your loss; my loss is your win." But the idea that a competitive move by one company invariably comes at the expense of another company puts forth a false dichotomy.

A zero-sum mentality led the German political philosopher Karl Marx to mistakenly think that the only way to keep profits high was to keep wages low. But while his rationale made perfect sense during the no-growth agricultural era of the 1820s, it fell apart a couple of decades later with the emergence of the techno-cultural economy. By the same token, a zero-sum mentality may have been a useful paradigm when the boundaries of a company were well-defined and impermeable, before massive amounts of data could be shared electronically over an open network. But again: What a difference a couple of decades can make!

To move beyond the zero-sum perspective, managers need to think in terms of how to expand the size of the pie, by optimizing the system as a whole. Such optimization means squeezing inefficiencies out of the entire system, and then dividing up the gains. Consider the new tune that Apple Computer began to hum in 1999, after nearly two decades of doing battle with Microsoft in the desktop PC market: "We have to let go of the notion that for Apple to win, Microsoft needs to lose," declared CEO Steve Jobs, who would see Apple's stock multiply several times over in the years to come. It's further testament to the fact that collaboration can lead to nonzero-sum outcomes, and a better way for companies to compete.

Collaboration. Partnerships. Trust. To make precision marketing a reality, companies need to capture and share customer data across the extended business network, work together to enhance the overall customer experience, further grow their customer relationships, and integrate their technology infrastructures, including their outsourced call centers and other points of customer contact. And, in many cases, they need to embrace the new degrees of freedom around business process outsourcing, by partnering with vendors that have in place the right sets of tools and capabilities.

5
FIFTEEN MINUTES
OF PRIVACY?

Andy Warhol talked about everyone getting fifteen minutes of fame. If we're not careful, everyone may end up with fifteen minutes of privacy.

—Peter Schwartz, Chairman,
Global Business Network

When Hillary Rodham Clinton went on the talk show circuit in the summer of 2003, following the highly anticipated publication of her personal memoirs, she repeatedly invoked a "zone of privacy" to explain, much to the scorn of her critics, why some matters in her life were simply nobody else's business. *Zone of privacy* is a term that we ourselves repeatedly invoke in this chapter, not as a way to dodge probing questions from the likes of Katie Couric and Barbara Walters, but in an attempt to make sense of the ongoing privacy debate that sits at the very heart of precision marketing. Our goal, however lofty, is to resolve the tension that persists between marketers and consumers, by offering a simple set of guidelines for developing a workable, enduring *privacy philosophy*. Note: We are not offering a template for privacy policy. Privacy policies are for corporate lawyers; privacy philosophies are for marketing leaders.

As we discussed in previous chapters, precision marketing relies on collecting, storing, manipulating, analyzing, and acting on customer data. A smart and progressive approach to privacy can be the key to unlocking the front door to customers' valued personal information. But a cavalier approach to privacy can have a company barred from the premises forever. And therein lies the crux of our discussion.

Today, the back doors to gathering customer data abound. Sometimes it seems that anyone and everyone with access to a customer database has become a certified list broker. Consider Golf-Serv, a provider of online golf content. Declaring itself "the leading conduit between golfers and companies that want to reach golfers," GolfServ rents its list of 60,000 "golf enthusiasts" to marketers eager to target this population with related merchandise offers. The list consists of people who, during the registration process on the GolfServ website, left unchanged the checked-by-default box that reads *I would like to receive special offers from GolfServ and its partners.* Every checked box increases the value of GolfServ's most valuable asset. Similarly, BlackPlanet.com rents its list of 1,832,844 African Americans. FastWeb rents its list of 5,708,909 education seekers. Novaparenting.com rents its list of 74,276 expectant parents (better hurry!). And so on. Some list aggregators trumpet their ability to reach tens of millions of e-mail prospects, selectable by age, income, number of children, marital status, geography, and so on, through their "proprietary consumer networks," while providing access to many more prospects through their "third-party relationships."

Yet one wonders: By having left unchanged that checked-by-default box on the GolfServ registration page, was Joe Consumer *really* saying, in essence, "Any friend of GolfServ is a friend of mine"? We discuss the cons of using third-party data later in this chapter. For now, suffice it to say that at its core precision marketing should be a front-door philosophy that aims to build healthy, sustainable relationships with the best prospects and customers, and that the only real way to architect these relationships is by *respecting* their privacy. It sounds so simple. "*R-e-s-p-e-c-t,* find out what it means to me," Aretha Franklin famously bellowed. What respect means to customers, and how companies can then implement this understanding in their marketing strategy, however, is often somewhat difficult to pin down.

For many marketers, the path to privacy appears potholed by myriad and often competing forces. With technological, legislative, and industry-specific variables in a constant state of flux, one could argue that creating a singular, meaningful privacy prescription would be an impossibly complex undertaking. Yet, taking a cue from Winston Churchill, who once observed that "Out of intense complexities intense simplicities emerge," we find that such a prescription is not nearly as complicated or convoluted as one might expect.

Given the current state of affairs, we believe that forward-thinking marketers really have only one, future-proof option: to embrace a privacy philosophy built around engaging their best customers in an ongoing dialogue, a first-person conversation where data is explicitly and freely exchanged in return for value. We call this scenario *the consensual customer*, and we discuss it at greater length as this chapter unfolds. But first, let's take a look at how we got here.

MARKETERS AS PEEPING TOMS

For most of us, the word *privacy* conjures up images of being left alone. We think of DO NOT DISTURB signs hung on hotel door-knobs to keep the maids from barging in. In contrast, many marketing tactics are, by their very nature, *intrusive*. TV ads interrupt programming. (That the ads also underwrite those same programs is a fact that's lost on many ad-skipping consumers and, as we suggest in Chapter 1, could become a major issue in the age of the DVR.) Merchandise catalogs sneak in amid the holiday greeting cards. Spam masquerades as personal e-mail (and now, by some estimates, accounts for some 45 percent of all e-mail traffic). And annoying pop-up ads do just what their name implies—now even on the miniaturized screens of wireless devices.

After decades of these multiplying intrusions, a growing number of consumers only wish that they could take refuge in a zone of privacy. (The government's do-not-call registry for blocking telephone sales pitches is testament to that fact, having grown to more than 28 million numbers within a month after its launch in June 2003.) The very notion of privacy has evolved into a catchall rallying cry aimed at stemming the rising tide of commercial interruptions and disarming the perceived evildoers.

But what exactly is meant by privacy? Again, in our mind's eye, privacy happens in seclusion, behind a closed door or a pulled shade. We talk of things being done or said *in* private. There's a notion that privacy somehow requires an enclosed space, a place where peering eyes are kept at bay by various protective measures, if not by a sense of propriety. So when we imagine our privacy being violated, we usually think of someone who is willing to break behavioral conventions to infiltrate our presumably secure and enclosed spaces. We even have a name to describe such a person: Peeping Tom. But alas, the original Peeping Tom could hardly be blamed for his voyeurism; and privacy expectations are often in the eye of the beholder.

According to legend, Tom was a tailor in the town of Coventry who, unlike other townspeople, refused to shutter his windows and avert his eyes on that fateful day when Lady Godiva wore a smile and nothing else on her gallop through town. After catching a glimpse of the lady in all her glory—violating her privacy, if you will—Tom was struck blind by a reproachful god. And so today "Peeping Tom" is used as a pejorative term, shorthand for those who are perceived to operate outside the rules of decency and invade the private space of others. That a naked woman was riding a horse through the center of town seems not to matter. Tom peeped, and so Tom paid.

This same sense of scorn now applies broadly to marketers who acquire and wield consumers' personally identifiable information, whether their Social Security numbers, their purchase histories, or simply their first names. In 2003, H&R Block found itself under fire for pitching various lines of financial services based on the information that taxpayers entered into their tax return forms using Free File, an electronic preparation and filing program. H&R Block defended its actions, stating that cross-marketing in this manner was perfectly acceptable, since consumers using the forms had already consented to receive information. Several large consumer groups begged to differ.

That consumers routinely behave like exhibitionist equestrians—filling out surveys in malls, entering farfetched sweepstakes, and clicking on all manner of reckless overtures from major companies and less-than-reputable firms alike—seems to many people to be beside the point. Marketers engaged in the collection of consumer data have all been painted with the same

Peeping Tom brush, no matter how complicit many consumers are in their own exploitation.

Through all the consumer caterwaul over privacy a simple fact remains: Marketers who don't quickly grasp the sensitive nature of consumer privacy concerns and who simply engage in data grabs are actually working against their stated objectives of retention, loyalty, and growth—and are driving customers, new and old, *away* from their products and services. As obvious as this statement may seem as you read it here—that marketers who antagonize customers will eventually lose them—it's apparently slow to sink in, especially for marketers of the direct persuasion. (And we've all heard the argument that, today, *all* marketers are direct marketers of one stripe or another.)

Consider the so-called Privacy Promise of The Direct Marketing Association (DMA), the largest trade association for businesses interested in direct, database, and interactive global marketing, with nearly 5,000 member companies. On its website, the DMA touts its Privacy Promise as "an important step for our industry." In our view, however, the promise represents a somewhat feeble attempt to respond to the consumer rallying cry. To summarize the Privacy Promise, DMA members basically agree to remind customers each year of their ability to opt out of future programs; to actually honor those requests when made; to allow customers to request placement on a suppression list to avoid future contacts across all channels; and to use DMA-provided tools to assure that suppressed customers are not contacted. While this promise is, admittedly, better than nothing, it leaves the customer in the tedious position of playing Whack-a-Marketer to fend off the advances of each new suitor.

The DMA puts the onus to opt in or opt out—that is, to give or to deny permission to be marketed to—squarely on the shoulders of the consumer. Meanwhile, there are many observers who remain convinced that the general public, with the exception of a small but vocal group of privacy zealots, remains deeply in the dark as to what all the fuss is about, in the first place—that, essentially, a vast majority of people are ignorant of the fact that marketers systematically compile and exploit their consumer data in practically every way possible. As Michael Doyle, representative from Pennsylvania, told a 2001 congressional hearing on privacy, ". . . most consumers don't have a clue how data is being collected on them. They don't understand what a cookie is; they don't know, when they are surfing the Web, what is happening to them. Trust me, they don't."[1]

It's no wonder the DMA and its member companies are happy to put consumers in charge of their own privacy. But what they may not yet realize is that it's not working. Ignorant customers may be less litigious, but they're not necessarily good customers. Market research data suggests that consumer concerns about privacy and security—including identity theft and credit card fraud—cause online retailers to lose billions of dollars a year. Jupiter Media Metrix forecasts that $24.5 billion in online sales will be lost by 2006 due to consumer privacy concerns, compared to an estimated $5.5 billion lost in 2001.

WHAT'S OLD IS NEW AGAIN?

"Today, privacy is more important to us than almost anything else," says Bill Mirbach, vice president of direct marketing at Intuit, the $1 billion-a-year financial software maker whose flagship products include QuickBooks, Quicken, and TurboTax. "You can't do effective marketing without putting super-effective privacy policies in front of it."[2] Mirbach didn't subscribe to this view only a couple of years earlier, when Intuit had few, if any, resources assigned to consumer privacy. But nowadays, the company is constantly refining its privacy policies in an effort to make them as watertight as possible. To that end, each business unit at Intuit has a "privacy advocate" whose job it is to work with the marketing managers to provide Socratic dialogue as they go about the day-to-day challenges of figuring out where the privacy line needs to get drawn. These privacy advocates report to a "privacy governing board" composed of senior executives, who meet once a month to hash out the relevant issues.

Although the growth of the Internet and database technologies for optimizing customer data has made consumer privacy seem like a wild and woolly frontier for even sophisticated software companies like Intuit, one can make the case that little has changed since 1967. Longtime Columbia University professor Alan Westin, now retired and leading the Center for Social and Legal Research, a public policy think tank that studies the issues of consumer privacy, remains the preeminent voice in the discussion on the intersection of privacy and business issues. His lean definition of the playing field rings as true today as it did nearly 30 years ago: "Privacy is the claim of individuals, groups, or institutions to determine for themselves when, how, and to what extent information about them is communicated to others."

Making one of his many appearances before a congressional committee focused on the subject of privacy, Westin testified that a "well-documented transformation in consumer privacy attitudes" has occurred over the past decade, resulting in more than 75 percent of American consumers becoming 'privacy assertive' in their dealings with commercial enterprise.[3] Indeed, privacy is a growing concern for consumers and marketers alike, despite *and* because of the fact that multiple and ongoing symposia, organizations, legislative efforts, and grassroots campaigns—too numerous to mention, let alone summarize—have done little to allay consumers' skittishness and curtail marketers' aggressiveness. The more things change, the more privacy remains the same: nettlesome, to say the least. Marketers crave efficiency while consumers demand autonomy.

And yet so much *has* changed. With the ubiquitous and forevermentioned advances in technology of the past three decades have come colossal opportunities for Westin's "individuals, groups, or institutions" to effect—and to suffer themselves—still greater assaults on privacy. Yes, the collection of consumer data online is just a new dimension of a very old practice. Yet the new dimension is fraught with potentially dire consequences for consumer privacy—and perhaps even civilization as a whole, if one believes, as the author Ayn Rand did, that "civilization is the progress toward a society of privacy." In this context, consumers' ongoing vigilance is not only understandable but well warranted.

Just recently, a major pharmaceutical manufacturer inadvertently disclosed the e-mail addresses for nearly 700 users of a leading antidepressant drug. While this is anomalous behavior—most privacy abuses are perpetrated by fly-by-night operations, not multinational corporations—it's enough to scare even the most laissez-faire consumer. Identity theft is also on the rise. In the United States alone, identity thieves steal more than half a million Social Security numbers each year.

Although the Internet seems to be the least personal of marketing's four doors to the consumer—after retail, mail, and the telephone—it's the one that has given rise to the greatest consumer privacy concerns. Perhaps that's because, at its inception, it seemed to offer the greatest potential for consumers to fly under marketers' radar and to be truly anonymous. Online adventurers called themselves "surfers," invoking the persona of wild-eyed, devil-may-care explorers who, while in cyberspace, could assume a level of anonymity that unlisted telephone numbers and NO SOLICITORS signs had been unable to afford them in the terrestrial world.

At first, consumers' primary fears were related to the security of their wallets. No matter how many times they heard the oft-invoked wisdom that their credit card numbers were safer transmitted via a Web form than their twenty-dollar bills were when being transmitted from pocket to palm, they still were slow to do their Christmas shopping over the computer. Even after a decade of online commerce, little more than one percent of retail purchases are consummated in cyberspace. In the age of clicks-and-mortar, the clicks are awfully quiet. Nonetheless, as consumers continue to spend more time on the Internet and gain more experience participating in online transactions, their initial reticence will give way to warm feelings of trust and comfort, right? Wrong. According to survey data from Odyssey, a San Francisco market research firm, despite the fact that most online consumers have been online for two years or more, they actually are becoming *less* comfortable about the security of their personal and financial information in online transactions.

If anything, according to Odyssey, consumers' Internet experiences are actually making it worse. Some 69 percent of all online users responding to a recent survey reported that one of their greatest concerns was that their personal data could "end up in the wrong hands." And among online purchasers specifically, these negative numbers are actually on the *increase*. Another recent survey revealed that nearly three-quarters of online users report a fear of misuse of personal data "holds them back a great deal" from making online purchases.

Oddly, in spite of all these ominous numbers, marketers and consumers each seem to dig more deeply entrenched positions. Although offering subtle language to the contrary, most marketers cling to the dream of unfettered access to consumer data, which they quietly justify by promising benefits like lower prices and less eventual pestering as the upside of sharing consumer data. ("If you don't want to hear from us, we don't want to spend money to reach you" is a common rhetorical refuge for the mass marketer draped in precision marketers' clothing. If the line were true, they'd simply stop buying lists from third-party data aggregators tomorrow. They have not.)

Meanwhile consumers seem to want as much privacy as possible, and they remain on the lookout for any attempts to manipulate their behavior or invade their inner sanctum. Oh, they still expect convenience, customization and low, low prices. But they'd seemingly prefer to receive these benefits from anonymous discount barns and folksy warehousers rather than from

191

familiar shopkeepers, the likes of which are all but extinct. Even progressive mom-and-pop shops that deign to start customer databases learn quickly that "your phone number, please" requests are usually met with expressions of disgust. "Let me in, I love you" is the rallying cry of the marketer; "Go away and value me" is the resounding reply from consumers. The challenge is to find ways to reconcile such diametrically opposed views.

While privacy has long been a hornets' nest of public concern, the current, Internet-enabled marketing climate is akin to grabbing that nest and shaking it repeatedly. "With the advent of online data collection, the American consumer's information privacy concerns have rightfully been heightened," were the understated words of the chairman of the Subcommittee on Commerce, Trade and Consumer Protection, in his opening remarks at the legislative hearing for the Consumer Privacy Protection Act of 2002.[4]

In an effort to appease consumers, federal and state governments, as well as professional standards bodies, have enacted and encouraged a broad and varied canvas of legislative and self-regulatory regimes, including:

Regulatory Requirements
~ Drivers Privacy Protection Act (DPPA)
~ Fair Credit Reporting Act (FCRA)
~ Children's Online Privacy Protection Act (COPPA)
~ Telephone Consumer Protection Act and Telemarketing Sales Rule
~ State Do-Not-Call Requirements
~ Census Confidentiality Act
~ State Voter Records Act
~ Gramm-Leach-Bliley Act
~ Equal Credit Opportunity Act (ECOA)
~ Fair Debt Collection Practices Act (FDCPA)

Self-Regulatory Standards

~ Direct Marketing Association (DMA) Privacy Promise

~ DMA Telephone Preference Service

~ DMA Mail Preference Service

~ DMA Electronic Mail Preference Service

~ DMA Ethical Guidelines

Many of these legislative and ethical constraints are aimed squarely at the major data aggregators whose data-suctioning tentacles seem to know no bounds. Again, in this context, recent congressional testimony is revealing, as demonstrated in the following exchange:[5]

REPRESENTATIVE CLIFF STEARNS, FLORIDA:

So I could come to you and say, okay, I want somebody who is making between $50,000 and $100,000 who is interested in rhythm and blues music, who enjoys skiing, who has a fishing license, and attends church, and is also interested in gardening, and is married with three children. You could come back with a list?

DEBORAH ZUCCARINI, EXECUTIVE VICE PRESIDENT AND CHIEF MARKETING OFFICER, EXPERIAN MARKETING SOLUTIONS:

We could come back with a list, yes.

MR. STEARNS:

And you would give me names?

MS. ZUCCARINI:

We would.

For companies whose core business is collecting, analyzing, and disseminating customer data, navigating these troubled waters is simply a cost of doing business. But for other companies, they represent a dangerously complex array of obstacles that threaten their ability not only to compete and prosper, but merely to survive.

The Information Technology Industry Council (ITIC), an association of leading IT companies, recently compiled a list of 20 privacy issues related to public concerns, balanced by a laundry list of Current Protections, ranging from technical fixes like anti-cookie software and browser settings to the Fourth Amendment to the U.S. Constitution, and Potential New Actions, ranging from pending legislation to stronger enforcement of existing laws. This inventory of privacy woes and their current and pending antidotes resembles nothing more than a complicated engineering flowchart, the likes of which are enough to make consumers and marketers alike simply give in to despair. Still, according to a recent survey by Consumers International, a worldwide federation of more than 260 consumer organizations, the United States' patchwork, self-policing approach is actually more effective at protecting consumer privacy than the seemingly more strident and uniform policy of the European Union.

A CABINET-LEVEL PRIVACY OFFICER?

Like Intuit, many companies are creating a flood of new positions focused on privacy matters. Many companies are also attempting to navigate this patchwork privacy regime by appointing yet another cabinet-level executive. Witness the emergence of the chief privacy officer (CPO), the business equivalent of a cabinet-level secretary of homeland security. (Just whom these executives are protecting remains to be seen.) In a perfect world, the CPO would emerge as the preeminent consumer advocate within any corporate fiefdom, the privacy-protector par excellence. Unfortunately this arrangement smacks of putting the proverbial fox in charge of the privacy henhouse. Thus far, the primary role of the CPO has been to catalog factors that include legislation, litigation, technology, and consumer choice, and to provide a warm, reassuring presence when called to testify before Congress.

Meanwhile spammers, identity thieves, and other privacy outlaws continue to resemble, well, terrorists. They're largely decentralized and wily, here today and gone tomorrow, and not particularly concerned with public opinion. While CPOs endeavor to help legitimate companies consolidate their privacy efforts in a single in-box, it remains to be seen whether they'll have any effect on decreasing privacy abuses—and increasing consumer trust—over the long haul. With a few notable exceptions, it's the data terrorists who perpetrate the most visible and storied privacy abuses. Some have even taken on nicknames like those given to infamous criminals. The recent apprehension of the Buffalo Spammer, the elusive upstate New Yorker who allegedly sent 825 million unwanted e-mails to unsuspecting consumers, is just the latest in a long line of stories about privacy outlaws that began with Peeping Tom and extends through hacker hero Kevin Mitnick, the gentleman (ahem) from Buffalo, and many others eager to wreak havoc on the world.

Still, as with the long lines we see in airports, it's the legitimate players that bear most of the brunt of prevention and vigilance. Unfortunately, the bad guys seldom wear those helpful black hats anymore, and spam-scams are increasingly difficult to discern from legitimate marketing campaigns. (Or, to embellish that popular *New Yorker* cartoon shown in Chapter 1, "On the Internet, nobody knows you're not a legitimate commercial enterprise.") As a result, congressional hearings have turned into lengthy digressions on how to balance the usual teeter-totter of consumer-protection legislation on the one side, corporate self-policing on the other. For now, most major marketers continue to favor self-policing, despite the fact that a lawless privacy frontier makes it tougher to distinguish good guys from bad.

Interestingly, for some people, the notion of absolute privacy is as antiquated as the house call or the telegram. "Get over it," says Sun Microsystems founder Scott McNealy. He has a point. We've all heard that the distributed computer networks that make up the Internet were engineered to be invulnerable to nuclear attack. But they are also proving nearly as impervious to legislation, litigation, or other traditional means of constraint. As Kevin Kelly famously wrote back in 1995, our default operating environment for the foreseeable future is not Windows, but simply "Out of Control."[6] And since privacy is all about *controlling* access to one's own personal data, perhaps consumers would do well to heed McNealy's admonition.

Fat chance. As the aforementioned data from Odyssey and Alan Westin indicate, consumers are not ready to surrender. For marketers, an attitude adjustment is in order. For an example of how a simple change in attitude can make a profound difference, we need only look to the evolving field of professional sales.

In the 1950s and 1960s, sales meant boots on the ground: a door-to-door salesman like the Fuller Brush man beaming at your doorstep or buttering up your receptionist. Then the 1970s saw the advent of catalog and telemarketing. But just as marketers have slowly adopted customer-centric, precision techniques, so, too, has a cultural change occurred for their nearest cousin, the salesperson. In the past two decades, we've witnessed the shift from an "invade and persuade" sales model toward so-called relationship- and solution-selling methodologies. Salespeople have learned that discerning prospects prefer to feel they're being serviced rather than sold. Savvy marketers would do well to heed this distinction.

Today, sales meetings are rife with discussions of customers' and prospects' pain points, implying a careful, considered, and analytical approach to treating and eventually curing the customer. Curiously, this language suggests entering a new privacy realm, too. We're used to freely dispensing our most precious, private information to the various professionals who populate the medical establishment. Why? Because, quite simply, it's the price of entry. And yet it's interesting to note that the health care arena is one of the few places where federal guidance is abundantly clear, via the Health Insurance Portability and Accountability Act of 1996 (HIPAA), which only recently took effect, and whose impact had yet to be felt as of this writing (although fear of noncompliance has already created something of a cottage industry for third-party "compliance partners").

Still, for the mass of marketers, the pursuit of any coherent privacy philosophy is one of quiet desperation. What's needed is a simple operating idea that at best allows marketers to fly above the fray of existing and pending legislation, and at worst keeps them from sinking into the morass of consumer distrust and paralysis.

THE DYNAMICS OF PRIVACY: THE WORLDS WE LIVE IN

During the writing of this chapter, there was little trouble collecting privacy failures, examples of how data and trust had been compromised in the name of unfettered commerce. Usually, the breaches were unwitting—or at least miscalculated. Perhaps the most prominent example involved JetBlue Airways, which in September 2003 admitted to having provided 5 million passenger itineraries to a Pentagon defense contractor, which then augmented that data with Social Security numbers and other personal profile information. The uproar was loud and immediate. Many other examples could be found in the daily news. What there was trouble finding were examples of privacy *successes*, tales of companies whose approach to privacy represents a clear and consistent model for marketers to follow.

Nonetheless, as we surveyed the evolving landscape of

privacy, spoke with experts, pored over transcripts of congressional hearings, surfed from one privacy advocacy website to another, and Googled phrases like "opt out," "privacy enhancing technology," and "privacy seals," we began to discern the characteristics of a deceptively simple road map for marketers to follow. The endpoint of that road map is what we call the consensual customer. In a nutshell, it describes a future where marketers more or less accept the inevitable: The best road is the high road.

As mentioned at the start of this chapter, the consensual customer scenario describes a world where forward-thinking marketers embrace a front-to-back privacy philosophy that focuses on securing customers who willingly engage in a first-person, ongoing exchange of data for value. It is, in fact, an opt-in-only world where customers are in the driver's seat, and where all major marketers follow the lead of visionary companies like Procter & Gamble. In describing P&G's overall approach to consumer privacy, Zeke Swift, the director of Global Privacy, noted that P&G strives "to treat information provided by individuals as their own, which has been entrusted to us, and we strive for transparency with consumers about how their information is used."[7]

Before we spend more time outlining the path to consensual customers, it's helpful to consider the dynamics that give rise to it. Marketers must choose their privacy philosophy across two major dimensions:

~ Who will collect and own customer data?
~ Will the data relationship be static and short-term, or dynamic and long-term?

Figure 5.1 plots these questions in a standard four-space framework and reveals three other scenarios that marketers are likely to see on the road to consensual customers.

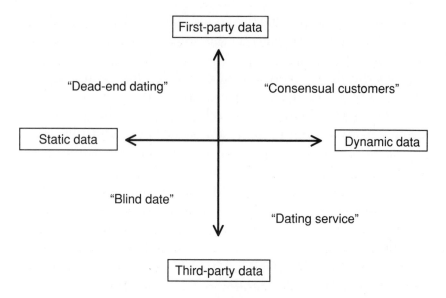

FIGURE 5.1   The Privacy Four-Space

THE *X* AXIS: WHERE IS THIS
RELATIONSHIP HEADED?

The *x* (horizontal) axis describes whether or not data is intended for limited use—say, one of those vacation sweepstakes drawings at the mall that creates an immediate call list for the local travel agent—or is collected as part of an ongoing campaign to profile prospects and customers and to create a lasting record. Amazon.com's extensive customer profiling, the product of an elaborate technical infrastructure that supports an extensible, customer-centric business philosophy, represents a world where the data relationship is engineered from the first to be dynamic and ongoing. (Paul Misener, Amazon's vice president for Global Public Policy, doesn't mince words about where the company stands in the debate: "Amazon is pro-privacy." Perhaps it's no coincidence that, in 2003, Amazon earned the highest score ever for a service company on the American Customer Satisfaction Index.)

On the other hand, the most visible and vociferous consumer privacy complaints arise from data that is acquired for short-term, limited use. Telemarketers selling anything from magazines to mortgages are usually working from single-use lists that contain static data. They generally lack the ability to evolve customer profiles in any meaningful way. The same can be said for the mass of unwanted direct mail and e-mail solicitations.

THE *Y* AXIS: WHO OWNS AND CONTROLS THE DATA RELATIONSHIP?

The *y* (vertical) axis describes who owns and controls the data relationship. First-party data is collected and owned by companies from their own customers for their own use. For example, the data collected by eBay when the company registers a new buyer or seller is first-party data.

Third-party data, on the other hand, is data that was collected by anyone other than the company that wishes to use it. If eBay were to purchase a list of e-mail addresses of subscribers to *Modern Quilt* magazine, for example, then the company would be buying third-party data. By the same token, if eBay were to provide its user data to the magazine, that data would become third-party data at the point at which it changed hands.

What's wrong with third-party data? After all, haven't marketers made successful use of list rentals and other third-party prospect data for decades? The answer, of course, is a resounding *yes.* But the answer to the first question—what's wrong with it—is perhaps even more resonant: *Customers don't like it.* To paraphrase Seth Godin's groundbreaking book *Permission Marketing,* providing your customer's data to a third party is like sending someone else out on a date with your girlfriend. It isn't just bad form. It's a relationship ender!

In the Introduction to this book we discuss how, in this era of promiscuous consumption, brand allegiance has given way to price-consciousness and convenience. This is perhaps a result of the fact that third-party data ownership and control has become commonplace, if not popular. Third-party data represents promiscuity. It's the business equivalent of a one-night stand. In contrast, first-party data is the stuff of going steady with the intention, assuming all goes well, to one day marry.

By further extending Godin's relationship metaphor, we can begin to conceptualize four dominant scenarios for how marketers can choose to acquire and evolve customer data. These scenarios—*Blind Date, Dead-End Dating, Dating Service,* and the *Consensual Customer*—are each described in the following sections.

BLIND DATE: A WORLD OF LIST BROKERS AND ONE-NIGHT STANDS

Blind Date is actually a generous name for this scenario, since a real-life blind date usually involves well-intentioned friends attempting to match two well-intentioned singles who, granted, often have little more in common than their singleness. (There's a reason that the term *blind date*, like Peeping Tom, usually evokes sneers and jeers.)

In the Blind Date scenario, static, third-party data is wielded in pursuit of marketing consummation. This is the world of list brokers and data aggregators, of anonymous sales drones mispronouncing customers' names and insulting their intelligence with random offers. Sure, there's a chance they'll get lucky, but there's also the chance that disaster will strike. Marketers whose privacy philosophy resides in the Blind Date quadrant are playing with fire.

DEAD-END DATING: A WORLD OF LIMITED INFRASTRUCTURE AND SERIAL MONOGAMY

Dead-End Dating is only slightly more desirable than the Blind Date scenario. In Dead-End Dating, marketers pursue first-party data—that is, they collect and own it themselves—without the plans or potential for evolving it. In this world, marketers typically are lacking in one or more of the following categories: technology, business processes, organizational capacity, and vision. Customer data is viewed only as a means to an end, and it's collected ad hoc and ad infinitum. Although they may pose as "customer-centric" companies, Dead-End marketers are really impostors, lacking as they do the infrastructure to share, evolve, and enhance the value of data across campaigns and channels. At first, these types of companies may seem nice enough. After all, they show up with a smile and they seem interested. But over time, they simply become pests. Sooner or later, customers come to realize that there's no future in a Dead-End relationship.

DATING SERVICE: A WORLD OF INFOMEDIARIES AND POLYAMOROUS LOYALTY

Dating Service is the world of the so-called *infomediaries*—data compilers and marketing partner alike, earnest third-party enterprises that are committed to maintaining robust, evolving customer data stores. While this is the best of the three scenarios we've described so far, it's far from perfect. Many infomediaries retain control over the data and the customer relationship, albeit in noninvasive fashion. One such example is iDine, the online rewards program that tracks customer transactions across a network of restaurants and hotels in exchange for various discounts. Another example is Gold Points, a subsidiary of Carlson Marketing Group, which essentially does the same thing across an even broader array of merchants.

202

Whether these low profile infomediaries can endure, and how many consumers will tolerate them remains to be seen (for its part, Gold Points appears to be going strong, with more than 8 million members). But unless this is your business, chances are the benefits to you are negligible at best. More likely is that these businesses are gaining new customers on your goodwill. For now, at least, this is a benign scenario.

THE CONSENSUAL CUSTOMER: A WORLD OF COMMITMENT

In the world of the Consensual Customer, consumers never have to worry about where their data is at night. Not unlike Lands' End's famous, "Guaranteed. Period." policy, which allows their customer to return any item at any time for any reason, the Consensual Customer is a privacy policy that says, "It's your data and you can have it back at any time."

Perhaps the best example of this philosophy comes from Procter & Gamble's Reflect.com, a personalized cosmetics business that places customer data squarely at the center of the business model. Their privacy philosophy leads their clear, easy-to-read privacy policy in large type: "We respect your privacy tremendously and will never share or sell your personal information—period." This, in a nutshell, reflects the simplicity of Consensual Customer. Respect. Never sell or share. Period.

Not surprisingly, Amazon does a nice job of demonstrating a Consensual Customer-like approach in the four privacy commitments that it makes to customers:

~ Notice (they were one of the first companies to actually publish a privacy policy).
~ Choice (customers always have meaningful and context-relevant opportunities to opt in or out, and to change their mind at a later date).

203

- ~ Access (customers can see the information Amazon has on them, and they can even alter or suppress certain data if they so desire).
- ~ Security (not only does Amazon respect customers' privacy, they're actively engaged in protecting it).

For companies intent on making similar commitments, and embarking on the path to a world of consensual customers, here are some other guidelines to keep in mind.

Lead with Your Privacy Philosophy.   Privacy policies are the legal documents that appear on the back of your sales collateral or on the bottom of your website. Privacy philosophies, on the other hand, are go-to-market statements about how you intend to service and value your customers over the long haul. One example of this is IBM's, which recently featured CPO Harriet Pearson in a series of print ads.

Communicate the Benefits of Information Liquidity.   When most of us think of the benefits of consumer data for marketers, we think in terms of what's right in front of us—the customized, personalized offers, higher conversion rates, and so on. But what we often fail to remember is the profound ripple effect of improved customer data across and beyond our organization— we're able to anticipate demand, improve customer service, lower prices, and so on. Customers must hear about these benefits and must be able to directly relate value and data. One way to achieve this is by empowering your contact center staff to communicate why they're asking for certain data and how that information will directly benefit the customer.

Grant Data Autonomy to Your Customers.   Simply stated, customers must be able to access, alter, and suppress their customer data.

Ask Only for What You Need. Early Internet marketing efforts were largely land grab exercises, where the ultimate metric of success was quantity not quality, new customers not good customers. That same gluttony characterizes much of marketers' historical approach to data collection. Why pursue and store your customer's hair color if you're in the oil change business?

Consider and Explain Context. Imagine you're walking down the street and a total stranger smiles at you and calls you by name. It's the stuff of horror movies and government conspiracies. It's also a primary tactic of aggressive direct marketers. Yes, personalization is one of the things consumers want. But even more important to them is to be free from surprises. When Amazon.com suggests a book to a customer, it also includes a small, text link that says "Why was I recommended this?"

Create the Sense of Private Space. Private places feel safe. There are doors and window shades, perhaps even security guards. Consider how you might reinforce a sense of privacy for your customers when they're being asked to share personal data. Perhaps you'll create a separate section of your website for customers to access and alter their personal data, pages devoid of promotional messages and one-time-only offers. Or maybe you'll revisit the hiring profile for your call center reps (CSRs) so that more professional-sounding CSRs are hired to handle privacy-intensive campaigns.

Hire a CPO: Chief Privacy . . . Ombudsman? Perhaps you're a large, multinational firm who already has a Chief Privacy Officer in place. But what about a Chief Privacy Ombudsman, an impartial third party whose primary responsibility is to evaluate your marketing efforts from the perspective of customer privacy?

History reminds us that privacy is a hot button that never entirely cools off. It seems that legislation, litigation, and technology will forever remain locked in a tug-of-war between privacy zealots and marketing terrorists. Somewhere in the middle are companies that aspire to become state-of-the-art precision marketers. What should these companies do in the face of the privacy debate? Follow Scott McNealy's advice: *Get over it.* And the only way to truly get over privacy concerns is to rise above them. Companies can start today, by espousing a privacy philosophy that emphasizes first-person, ongoing, and consensual relationships between the organization and its customers. This simple gesture will lead to a place beyond legal and technological twists and turns. All that's left is customer choice. And for precision marketers, that's all that really matters, anyway.

6
THE PRECISION
MARKETING FUTURE

We looked at trends in mass-market culture in place today, and took them to their limit—creating a world where omnipresent, one-to-one advertising recognizes you and sells directly to you as an individual.

— Alex McDowell, production designer,
Minority Report[1]

The year is 2054, and major marketers have it easy. As biometric retinal scanners read the eyeprints of passersby in a streamlined supermall, interactive billboards greet them by name, pitching customized offers based on their individual customer profiles. These profiles contain voluminous data about their past purchase and interaction behavior across multiple retailers; their personal preferences, both articulated and unarticulated; their psychographic makeup along myriad dimensions; who they are, where they're going, and what they may wish to buy at that very moment in the context of their specific wants, needs, and situations.

"Good afternoon, Mr. Yakamoto," calls out a Gap employee from a large, flat-screen monitor. "How did you like that three-pack of tank tops you bought last time you were in?" The towering image is all smiles as she awaits the customer's response. In this case, of course, the customer is none other than John Anderton, the character played by Tom Cruise in the 2002 Steven Spielberg movie *Minority Report*.

The scene is just one of many scenes in the movie that depict technology-mediated, ultrapersonalized selling in an advertising-saturated environment. Consider a subway ad, which calls out: "John Anderton, you look like you could use a Guinness." Later in the movie, Anderton, on the run from his own law enforcement authorities, encounters an American Express billboard. The billboard displays each passerby's name on an oversized credit card, with the Member Since field dynamically updated to reflect each cardholder's membership status. "It looks like you need an escape," it remarks as Anderton passes within earshot, "and Blue can take you there."

"It's precision marketing," notes Jeff Boortz, founder of Philadelphia-based Concrete Pictures and creative director for the 14 full-fledged commercials, as well as many of the shorter spots interspersed throughout *Minority Report*. "People are shown ads only for those products they may actually want to buy."[2]

According to Boortz, the filmmakers had originally envisioned a world in which the ads would not only recognize consumers based on their individual profiles, but also on their individual states of mind. Marketers could target consumers to buy some product or service based on how they were *feeling* at that particular moment in time or on some measure of their emotional state—even, perhaps, on their overall biorhythmic readings. A company could essentially plug itself into people's mood rings and deliver customized marketing messages in response to the color of the display. And maybe deliver free therapy sessions, to boot!

Spielberg and his team, which in this case included 23 renowned futurists who assembled for three days to visualize the socio-technical landscape of a major metropolitan area 50 years hence, paint both a vivid and fascinating portrait of precision marketing. For many people, however, the portrait is also somewhat unsettling, given the wholesale erosion of personal privacy, as evidenced by the billboards that broadcast customer information for all the world to see and hear. (Of course from a script standpoint, the approach serves the narrative structure well, with its exploration of the ideas of choice, predestiny, and anonymity as a social construct that fails to exist in the media scheme of the future.)

The Hollywood version of precision marketing is largely extrapolative. It's firmly grounded in kernels of reality, drawing heavily from the potentialities that reside in today's emerging marketing and media technologies—some already deployed in some shape or form, and others on the verge of being launched. "Many of the capabilities we projected to show up in fifty years will more likely show up in 5 years," concedes Boortz. "Technology is advancing faster than anyone could have possibly anticipated."[3]

By 2015, predicts Bethesda, Maryland-based World Future Society, magnetic-strip ID cards will be replaced by biometric scanning (although retinal scanning may be out of the question, since sunglasses can block more that just UV rays). Other technologies that would enable the precision marketing future a la *Minority Report* include Web-based cookies, GPS and Bluetooth-enabled devices, DVR functionality, bar code scanners, location enabled networks (LENs), organic light-emitting diodes (OLEDs), and radio frequency ID (RFID) tags—tiny microchips that respond to a radio query by wirelessly transmitting a unique ID code, and that can be easily and cheaply embedded into practically any type of merchandise. The tags could also be embedded into wearable items such as key chains, credit cards, and wristwatches.

Perhaps more than any other technology currently on display or in development, the proliferation of RFID tags could have an enormous and immediate impact as an enabler of in-store precision marketing. After all, it gives retailers the potential to know who their customers are, pulling up their personal profiles the moment they set foot in the door. Imagine: The Gap links the RFID tag in your T-shirt with its purchase file. Suddenly, up comes a complete record of your past interactions and transactions with the store. Now the Gap could serve up all manner of customized offerings, no retinal scanners required! In terms of technology, the scenario isn't so farfetched, based on today's fast-evolving capabilities.

In reality, however, the scenario is unlikely to play out any time soon. The reason has everything to do with the American Civil Liberties Union, along with a host of other privacy advocates, that warn that such technologies could ultimately allow "corporations or the government to constantly monitor what individual Americans do every day."[4]

In 2003, these organizations successfully lobbied to put an end to experimental initiatives then underway by various companies to create RFID-based inventory control systems, designed to increase efficiencies in the supply chain and also root out shoplifting. In response to Big Brother concerns that retailers would monitor products long after consumers had purchased them and taken them home, several RFID chip manufacturers pledged to incorporate a "kill switch" to disable the tags at the checkout counter. So far, however, the move has failed to alleviate consumer fears—opposition to RFID tags even prompted Wal-Mart, that $250 billion retail behemoth, to cancel its planned trials of the new technology—perhaps due, in part, to a lingering sense of paranoia wrought by *Minority Report*!

The hornet's nest of privacy issues aside, at least for the moment, the ability to realize any semblance of the *Minority Report* vision from a technology standpoint would also depend on the advent of real-time channel, campaign, and analytics management systems. In essence, these systems would translate into a turbocharged version of the customer-facing applications suite (CFAS) we outline in Chapter 3, combined with a customer relationship repository (CRR) that transcends company-specific boundaries.

Indeed, one of the most intriguing aspects of the precision marketing future according to *Minority Report* is this very notion of a global customer database, or what we might call a Universal Customer Relationship Repository (UCRR). Again, interactions and transactions across multiple merchants would be recorded in the same repository—which, in turn, could be broadly accessed, as opposed to being tied to any one particular store. Walk into the Gap, for example, and a sales rep might offer you styles and colors to match the purse and shoes you just purchased at a different store. The idea is frightening—or is it? Loyalty rewards programs such as Gold Points, a subsidiary of Minneapolis-based Carlson Marketing Group, already capture customer data across multiple merchants. And, of course, credit card companies have been doing the same thing for years, even if they are explicitly prohibited from capitalizing on the mountain of transaction information.

Consider the UCRR applied in the context of moviegoing. First, imagine the multiple points of contact that major marketers have with customers throughout the course of a typical moviegoing experience, from selecting the movie, to buying the tickets using a credit card, to buying various food and drink items at the concession stand. More importantly, consider the paid product placements that continually pop up throughout the actual movie. The rate of product placements has dramatically increased in recent years, as has the price that marketers are willing to pay to have their products make a cameo appearance in a feature film production. (Steven Spielberg reportedly sold $25 million in product placements in *Minority Report*, for such brands as American Express, Reebok, and Pepsi. Lexus alone paid $5 million to put a futuristic car into the film—one that the moviegoer would never even have a chance to buy.)

Now, consider how, with the advent of the UCRR, major marketers might begin to capitalize on the transactions and interactions that transpire over the course of the moviegoer's experience. For example, Barnes & Noble might automatically serve up an offer to buy the related book or soundtrack. Or the Sports Authority might serve up an offer to buy a new pair of Reeboks. Or the local dealership might serve up an offer to test-drive a shiny new Lexus SC 430 convertible, the modern-day comparable of the model that Tom Cruise drove in *Minority Report* (or a Mini Cooper, for those who attended theatrical viewings of the 2003 remake of *The Italian Job*). To date, marketers have had no real means by which to track the effectiveness of their product placement programs—which, incidentally, are growing even more rapidly in television, as the traditional 30-second advertisement becomes less and less effective. With access to UCRR data, marketers could combine brand-exposure interactions with existing customer profile information to present personalized messages to qualified prospects.

In the end, the year 2054 will come and go without law enforcement officials having acquired the ability to arrest citizens before they commit a crime—the basic premise of the movie. Major marketers, on the other hand, will certainly have acquired the ability to present willing customers with just-in-time, context-sensitive offers long before that date. As we've discussed, the possibility is already being realized to varying degrees by a growing number of companies eager to enhance the profitability of their customer relationships—suggesting that, in the years ahead, precision marketing is sure to surprise us in ways that Hollywood has not yet even begun to imagine.

FINDING INSPIRATION IN *STAR TREK*?

In their relentless efforts to catch a glimpse of Tomorrowland, and help feed people's insatiable obsession for knowing "what's next," futurists often look for signs of explosions that may be looming just over the horizon. But alas, there are other ways for the Earth to move. Consider the way a steady stream of water wears a groove in stone, or the slow and massive overhaul that takes place as a glacier crawls imperceptibly across rocky terrain.

Big explosions make big noises, and the Internet was an explosion whose shock waves are still radiating. But perhaps much of what will drive future change in media and marketing will occur far more subtly. Perhaps it will be less revolutionary and more evolutionary, a natural outgrowth of trends already firmly in place. As technological and economic forces meet up with sociological changes, as they do battle and make love and create that mongrel spawn we call *reality*, perhaps what we'll see will be not so dramatic and charged as *Minority Report*, but something more nuanced and integrated—like, dare we say, the old *Star Trek* TV series.

Because in Kirk, Spock, Bones, and Scotty, what did we encounter but basic human archetypes wielding technologies that were deceptively simple on the surface and yet implied uncanny intelligence operating underneath? They were us! Those devices were our devices on steroids! The ship's sensors that Spock relied on? Well, maybe they were something like X10 remote control cameras linked up with Google. The phaser? Just a stun gun engineered by Nokia. And the communicator? Chances are, you can find a more advanced model right now in your very own pocket.

214

With that perspective in mind, we tend to think that the future will look an awful lot like the present. But of course it will be better integrated, with more distributed and seamless intelligence. Like *Star Trek*, minus the beaming. Personalization will be transformed from a thing of evil portent to a harbinger of freedom and *enhanced* privacy. Technology will indeed become ubiquitous, interoperable, miniature, and organic, as promised in practically every corporate vision video of the past two decades. Business and social culture will finally and fully release the vestiges of data silos, org charts, and privacy mania and begin to truly embrace creativity, collaboration, and the free flow of information. And people will walk around wearing blue pajamas and using neck pinches to paralyze assailants. (Just kidding.)

In our view, the future of precision marketing could very well come to resemble one or more of the three scenarios we put forth in the boxed sections that are threaded through the pages that follow. While we strove for originality, the scenarios are not unlike some of those that experts in the wireless industry have been batting around for several years in their efforts to create common cognitive ground, if only for the benefit of the investor community. In doing some time-traveling of our own, we simply aim to take these scenarios to the next logical level, and to frame them within the specific context of precision marketing.

Some of the scenarios are built upon the foundation of location-based services that use "presence and availability" protocols. These services, already in the early stages of being launched, rely on wireless networks that proactively poll for presence information about select mobile users, and determine whether these users are able and willing to let certain marketers reach them with proximity-sensitive messages. When it comes to precision marketing, these services open up a whole new world of possibility.

One commonly-evoked scenario involves passing by a Starbucks and receiving a text message on your cell phone from a computerized customer relationship system. It might read: "Come inside, and we'll give you 50 cents off a Caramel Macchiato!" The message is accompanied by a bar code that serves as a digital coupon. In this case, Starbucks recognizes that not only do you happen to be physically present just around the corner from one of its café locations, but you're also a loyal customer with a weak spot for expressos. With respect to privacy, you had already given Starbucks permission to send these types of special offers under a specific, predefined set of conditions (only on weekday afternoons and only within the city limits). And so you enjoy your vente Macchiato, having received an automatic credit to your loyalty program account. Meanwhile, Starbucks can revel in the fact that it leveraged its technology capabilities to make the cash register sing, when it would have otherwise remained silent.

Of course the notion of "presence and availability" in many ways speaks to the very precepts of the consensual customer that we outline in the previous chapter. After all, it's the mobile user—as opposed to the marketer—who's charged with setting the parameters around contact and privacy. *They* determine *when, where*, and *how* they want to be reached. Moreover, they decide *who* is and isn't allowed to reach them.

Short-term, the most common application of location-based technology has been Buddy List-like instant messaging capabilities that let friends and family know when you're in the general vicinity and willing to be contacted by them. (While AT&T wireless was the first U.S. carrier to launch the service—aptly called Find Friends—location-based services will likely be available to all 145 million wireless subscribers by 2005.) "Come over for dinner," pleads the recurring message from your mother. "You're only 3 miles away; we'll see you in 12 minutes."

Soon enough, the same principle will be extended to mobile commerce. Marketers are sure to have a field day discovering new ways to leverage the technology as they track customers' whereabouts and send them offers geared not only to their personal preferences but also to their location and present circumstances. "Hey, don't go to that gas station," bellows an urgent voice on your car's ad messaging system. "You can fill up your tank for five bucks less just around the corner. Stop by now, and we'll throw in a free car wash!" At this point, the promise of just-in-time marketing will have been fulfilled.

Finally, what about the "talking billboards" technology that figures so prominently in *Minority Report*? Is it all just pure fantasy? Well, even if interactive billboards were able to identify individuals at a distance using, say, RFID tags, calling out to a crowd of passersby would be not only highly intrusive and inappropriate but also impractical and even downright confusing. (Imagine a voice calling out to you and a hundred other people all at the same time!) Mass marketing and precision marketing are like oil and vinegar. Each serves a distinct purpose. To attempt to combine the two, by displaying personal information in a public setting (as opposed to, say, the privacy of your car), would probably never sit well with consumers.

That said, one wonders: Are we projecting whether people will accept this kind of invasion, and how they will behave in response to it, based simply on our present understanding of their behavior? Are we, once again, simply prisoners of what we know? Some people would argue that privacy concerns are a moving target. The social norms that govern these concerns are bound to change dramatically in the future as customers come to terms with the fact that, like it or not, they basically leave an electronic trail wherever they go. True, privacy legislation will ensure that "shadow marketing" is always carried out with permission, and on an opt-in basis. It's also probably true that, over time, a growing number of people will choose to stay permanently plugged in, provided the value exchange makes it worth their while. No doubt, adoption will skew demographically, as it always has. Already, the younger set has shown itself to be all about open communication. Teenagers, in particular, have a natural aptitude for being able to rapidly process the different types of messages they receive, and they have fewer qualms about sharing information that would allow marketing messages to be contextualized to their specific wants and needs.

With respect to talking billboards, the ideal model must be one that the consumer chooses, as opposed to one that is forced upon them. It should function on a pull rather than push basis—and, again, the information should be displayed privately rather than publicly. Today, a number of companies are developing innovative designs that conform to these criteria. In most cases, the designs allow consumers to point their PDAs or other devices equipped with an infrared port at a small electronic tag attached to a billboard or any other information display surface to download additional information and other content items, including games and coupons. Or how about one-click access to Web pages? A number of companies, including U.K.-based Hypertag, are pioneering the new technology. A trial version directed moviegoers to websites where they could download music, trailers, or stills from the movie. Of course, the technology allows content providers to present information tailored to the exact location of the user, opening up myriad possibilities in the context of practically any product or service.

FUTURE SCENARIO #1: GREET ME IN ST. LOUIS

You're in St. Louis on a business trip. Your meeting wraps up early, and your client suggests you check out the West End. "Lots of great bookstores and coffee shops over there," she tells you. "You'll love it."

You've never been to St. Louis, but you're not worried. Your rental car has a SmartGPS system integrated into the dash, so you simply say, "West End" to it and a map with driving directions pops right up. Woven into the map interface are clickable offers for hotels located nearby—the car, after all, knows you're a business traveler—and the most prominent of those offers is for the chain where you stay most often. Their offer features your name, your loyalty club balance info, and a customized offer: "You're almost there, Mr. So-and-So. Stay just one more night with us and enjoy a three-day stay at our new property in Cancun!"

You click the Ads Off button on the interface, knowing that you've just incurred an additional service charge for doing so. Who cares, though. You're on business. It's not your money.

Still, you saw the ad, and so you drive to the West End with Cancun on your mind. Maybe you'll stop by a bookstore to grab a Cancun travel guide, then sit at a coffee shop for a while and flip through it. Sounds like a plan.

You find a parking spot almost right away—the SmartGPS system alerts you there's one open on Euclid—and you're on foot. You flip open your cell phone. Well, that's what you call it, at least. But it's way more than a phone. It's a GPS system, a smart wallet, an e-mail device, a pager, a half-decent digital camera, an MP3 player, your day planner, and so forth. It's also an active filter for all the cellular packets that float invisibly through the ether. It knows your profile—as much as you want it to know—and it's ready to find offers that hit your sweet spot, if and when you let it. You're ready to turn it loose.

"Ads on," you say to it. "Bookstore."

Up pops a list of four bookstores within a quarter-mile radius of where you parked. One has a small, twirling dollar-sign icon next to it, and you tap on it with your finger.

"First-time customers take 20 percent off all magazines. Spend more than $30 and get a free travel tote."

The phone knows you're hundreds of miles outside your home service area, that you're not registered as a customer of that store—and so the savvy local bookseller has crafted a great offer for people like you. You quickly double-check to make sure they have a Travel section, and finding that they do, you get directions. As you're walking there, you say, "Coffee."

Bingo. Your favorite coffee shop has a location just two doors down from the bookshop. You can use your business debit account there straight off the phone. But wait a sec—there's another coffee shop listed next, and it also features an agitated icon vying for your attention. You stop for a second—walking while messaging has become a pretty major social faux pas these days, and everybody has a story of a head-on collision with a distracted cell-phone jockey—and you click the second coffee shop.

WE WANT YOU! We're working hard to win more customers like you, men 24–35 who drink specialty coffee at least five times a week. Stop by our West End store in the next hour and fill out a 60-second survey and any coffee drink you want is on the house.

You're feeling a little guilty about turning the ads off in the car, so this is perfect. Instead of expensing the mocha malt shake, you'll get it free. Right after you pick up your Cancun travel guide, a copy of the *Sports Illustrated* swimsuit issue, and the latest hardcover from your favorite fiction writer. That stuff will all fit nicely in your complimentary travel tote. . . .

FUTURE SCENARIO #2: DESTINATION STORES

Job interviews always make you nervous. But when you saw the ad crawling across the bottom of your TV last night, you just had to drag it into your SAVE folder. You were starting to think it was time to reformat your job agent, and then this one came in. It sounded almost too good. You e-mailed your resume this morning, and now you're riding the train downtown for an interview. You bring the ad up on your handheld—everybody's just calling it a handheld these days, because calling it a phone is like calling your car a chair—and you read it again:

RETAIL EXPERIENCE—ARCHITECT—CHICAGO

Leading skateboard manufacturer seeks creative individual to design personalized retail experiences for our upcoming department store launch. Ideal candidate will know skateboarding firsthand and will have some history of competition and/or heavy recreational experience. Will work closely with graphic designers and programmers to create super-kiosks that link directly to our corporate servers in New York. Will consider computer-savvy visual merchandisers willing to partake in our famous Experience Architect Bootcamp program. E-mail only. No calls or direct IR transmissions will be considered.

You're pretty sure you know what they're talking about. They must be part of the new SuperFields program, where old-line department store Marshall Field's is converting all their existing floor space into these bionic sales kiosks. Computer-driven audio and video presentations, interactive and clickable and friendly, customized to evolve according to prospects' interests and purchase histories. Within the past few years, all the old retailers have started programs like these.

Over time, it's become clear that people just like to shop—they like to congregate in places like Chicago's Michigan Avenue for the day, walk around, make whimsical purchases, and eat whimsical snacks.

Once giant generalists like Field's got the message, they realized all was not lost. People still liked to come to Field's. They wouldn't be losing all their business to online-only retailers like Amazon anytime soon. (In fact, there was talk that Amazon was actually looking into Michigan Avenue real estate.)

But retailers like Field's finally got it: If they wanted to actually consummate sales, they would need to reengineer their entire shopping experience. First off, consumers needed to be able to execute price and feature comparisons right there on the sales floor. Although many had personal devices—handhelds, cell phones, whatever you call them—to facilitate this process, the retailers added Internet terminals—even, in some cases, custom comparison engines that arrayed feature sets and prices in easy-to-read matrices—to make it easy for everyone. Their reasoning was simple: Customers required this information to consummate a purchase, and if they were going to do it anyway, retailers wanted to have at least some control over how they did it. Besides, retailers surmised, if customers won't buy until they have all the information, then it's my business to put all that information right there at their fingertips. Short of doing that, I'm shooting myself in the foot.

You read about all this on your portal page a few weeks back. You've been seeing a lot more business stories now that you've clicked the "unemployed and looking" tag on your profile. For the most part, the Field's business had become a service business: Maintain clean, technology-friendly, customizable retail space and lease it out to companies who see the benefit of aggregating their product alongside other like products. The more these companies pay, the better equipped their space is.

You hoped the skateboard company would invest in one of the more tricked-out stalls, or maybe even a whole corner of the store, with embedded flat-panel displays and ambient speakers built into the walls and ceiling and floor. And to really sell a skateboard, you needed to have a place for kids to ride. A simulator at the least, but preferably a real-live halfpipe with old-school coping glued across the top for effect. You could give lessons there, run demos, and even let people try out different equipment combinations before they bought anything. It would be a cinch to grab e-mail addresses from the corporate mothership and start some kind of "invitation only" program for prospective and current customers. And you could build customer profiles all day long by simply requiring shoppers to give data and fill out surveys in exchange for free skate sessions, custom T-shirt designs, and so forth.

Sure, it would be expensive to build all that stuff, to make it safe, and to buy appropriate insurance. But it would probably be a cinch to find a partner, a presenting sponsor, to partially or completely underwrite it. Heck, you'd be happy to give a sports drink company a little concession business, and your old pal at the helmet manufacturer would probably build the halfpipe in a heartbeat, as long as you did an exclusive with them. If the money was right, you'd even let them put a customer kiosk or two in your space.

You started making notes to prep for your interview. You didn't feel so nervous anymore.

FUTURE SCENARIO #3:   AGGREGATING ENTHUSIASM

When you were younger, you wanted to be an entrepreneur. True, you thought it was a French word that had something to do with mountain climbing, but still . . .

In college, your band had really started to build a following, and before you knew what happened you'd signed a record deal and hit the road. No entrepreneuring for you. You were a rock star!

Then the accident happened. Your bass player crashed the van, and although nobody was hurt, your other three band members decided that it was God's way of telling them to grow up and find real jobs.

After the band broke up, that's when you really got big. The critics wrote fawning pieces, talking about how you were really the star of the band and imploring you to get back in the studio. You wanted to do it, but you had a family now, not to mention a mortgage, student loans, and a small mountain of credit card debt you had racked up during the leaner days. And since the record company had screwed you royally, well, you weren't seeing dime one of royalties. Lame.

But then this website thing happened. Incredible. Somebody started Howzabout.com, a simple community where people could come together and commission new projects and products in the hope of bringing them to life.

You'd received an e-mail:

HOWZABOUT YOU WRITE SIX SONGS?

We're writing to tell you that more than 2,900 people have pledged a total of $30,000 to commission you to write and record at least six new songs by the end of the year. Home recordings and acoustic arrangements are okay. If you choose to accept this commission, please click the YES button below, and a representative of Howzabout.com will call you to initiate a contract.

No way. You figured it was real, though, because you had read about it recently. "Aggregated enthusiasm" was the buzzword of the day, the name given to a handful of websites that had sprung up to serve as wish-fulfillment brokerages. The premise was simple: Across the country and around the world, pockets of motivated consumers could band together to pledge things into existence. Neighborhood groups were commissioning new parks. Pranksters were offering thousands of dollars to convince a local politician to shave his head for charity. Tarantino announced plans to finance his next film entirely on Howzabout.com. And a group of nostalgia buffs in Boise had raised nearly a million dollars to convince Coke to bring back the old 16-ounce bottle to their leading grocery chain.

And now this: They wanted to underwrite your comeback. No record label. No ugly cross-country van tour. You could record at home in your spare time. And if things went well, maybe they'd commission six more songs after that.

You started thinking about the contract. Must get the rights to the e-mail addresses of the people who pledged, as many as possible. Could probably sell those old tour T-shirts for a premium. . . .

THE FUTURE OF CUSTOMER LOYALTY PROGRAMS

"Only Hilton Hhonors gives you airline miles and hotel points, and other rewards programs an inferiority complex," reads the caption for a new print ad. It features the photo of a Great Dane towering over a tiny lapdog whose nervousness is palpable. The implication, of course, is that any company without a solid rewards program in place should be highly intimidated by the "airline miles and hotel points" that Hilton Hhonors now offers its customers. But should such companies suffer from an inferiority complex? What's the future of customer loyalty programs, anyway? Certainly, it's an aspect of the current discussion that merits attention.

In our view, customer loyalty programs have an extremely bright future. But when we envision that future, what exactly are we seeing? It's not *Minority Report*. Again, fueled by technological advances, enhanced personalization, and degraded privacy protections, the movie places us in a scene where public space has become a gauntlet of aggressive, invasive marketing tactics that few consumers of today would enjoy, let alone tolerate. It presents a world where intrusion and persuasion remain the prevailing methods for marketers wishing to gain greater share of their targets' attention and wallets. In fact, after you have viewed the movie it's hardly a leap to imagine a talking end-cap corralling a hapless shopper with a Don Rickles-style come-on: "You with the cold sore! Get over to aisle seven before that thing explodes! Sale on Blistex!"

Hollywood is given to hyperbole and obliged to create narrative structures that depict tension and conflict. In presenting a scene out of marketing's future, Spielberg and his team obviously placed a premium on what is explicit and perhaps even controversial, as we already suggested. Real-life precision marketers, on the other hand, should be thinking in the opposite direction as they consider the future direction of their loyalty programs. Again, their goal should be to conceive and deliver marketing programs that are compact and consensual, that visit consumers at a time, and via a means, of their choosing.

These new loyalty programs, as they emerge, will likely be a good deal more boring than the ingredients that your average filmmaker requires to hold audience interest. In fact, these programs will more likely be quiet amalgamations of internal and implicit calculation, with companies and customers engaged in minute exchanges of information and value within the course of a traditional transaction. What's different and interesting about the customer programs will occur beneath—rather than on—the surface. While the programs would make for dull filmmaking, they will indeed make for exciting and rewarding commerce.

While subtle forms of the old "invade and persuade" strategy will continue to be used by new market entrants or by old-line marketers in search of new customers, loyal customers will seek and in fact expect refuge from this constant barrage of enticements. It's quite likely that, in the future, customer loyalty programs will become these zones of refuge.

As marketers learn more about consumers' preferences, there's less need to undertake dire, spastic schemes to hijack their attention. And as customers divulge more personal data

and engage in more two-way communication with their preferred brands, they're much less likely to expect, let alone tolerate, these practices.

For years, marketers conceiving customer loyalty programs
have focused on more, more, more. Marketers seem to be thinking, We'll get *more* information from our most loyal customers,
and then we'll give them *more* service, make *more* offers, create
more personalized communications, and reach out to them
through *more* touchpoints. If this is what they get for being loyal
and sharing information, many customers may actually choose to
opt out of loyalty.

A better scenario is that loyal customers will come to expect
fewer and better interactions. It's like what an old friend once
told us after growing annoyed by the onslaught of two-for-one
Pizza Pizza offers: "The pizza makers don't get it. I don't want two
bad pizzas. I just want one good one." Loyal customers harbor
this same resentment toward gimmicks. They just want one good
pizza. That's why they became loyal in the first place.

In the future, we expect that wise precision marketers will
resist the urge to build a large loyalty franchise that exceeds
the bounds of their normal customer interactions. Where old-
line loyalty programs often become empires in and of themselves, with magazines and clothing and advertising campaigns
engineered around them, newer programs will be invisibly
etched into the face of the business itself. They will be the
product of continuous data acquisition, ongoing and real-time
customer analysis and segmentation, and powerful and immediate offers and benefits delivered within the context of a normal customer interaction.

Amazon.com offers one sterling example of what loyalty programs of the future might look like. Loyal customers become co-
creators of what might be called a "loyalty environment," where
their entire browsing experience represents the sum total of their
ongoing relationship with the online retailer. Each page they're
served is constructed uniquely for the loyal, cookied customer.

Each time a customer shops at Amazon.com, he's making an investment in building a better shopping experience the next time.

Whether it's the various "store" tabs you're shown or the unique offers presented to you, Amazon has mastered the art of the invisible loyalty program. Each compressed moment of content you're served represents Amazon's best guess at what you're interested in. The more you surf and click—the more you share your preferences—the more your environment is tailored to your unique interests.

Even better, the entire operation is an open book to the customer, who is able to turn the various switches of customer preference on or off at will. Did you buy a certain book about sexual techniques that doesn't represent your usual reading habits? You have the option to tell Amazon's inference engine (the little program that's constantly measuring your buying habits, in the aggregate, against other Amazon shoppers in order to make more relevant recommendations) to ignore that purchase.

The next generation of recommendation engines—sometimes referred to as "guided-selling software"—promises even greater degrees of accuracy in terms of understanding the wants and needs of a customer in advance of serving up a specific product or service. Consider a technology platform developed by Cambridge, Massachusetts-based ChoiceStream. Unlike traditional personalization technologies based on clickstream or activity analysis, the ChoiceStream platform focuses on understanding the underlying attributes of the content and products being personalized, as well as users' preferences for those attributes. Armed with this insight, it then aims to align each user with the content or offerings that most closely matches their specific tastes and preferences.

Whatever the means, there's little doubt that most companies will continue to acquire more valuable and accurate data about their best customers. Particularly within the confines of loyalty programs—most of which exist to reward and entice customers who, in return, continue to exchange data with the corporate mother ship—marketers will gain increasing opportunities to acquire and utilize personal data. Since these valuable customers will quite likely be the treasured assets of more than one commercial enterprise, they will become quasi-celebrities of commerce. We see it already. The same consumers are bombarded with the bulk of direct-mail solicitations, catalogs, and other enticements. Assume a mortgage, buy a luxury car, apply for a credit card, and you've made the target prospect list for dozens if not hundreds of businesses.

But when it comes to celebrities, there's a fine line between awkward familiarity and harassment. To a celebrity customer, old school direct marketers will be perceived as stalkers; precision marketers, on the other hand, will be perceived as the subtle, helpful concierge at their favorite hotel.

Like celebrities, though, these consumers are more often leery of strangers calling them by name. What they really want is to be afforded a measure of anonymity, a pretense of formality, even. Perhaps your best customer would like nothing more than to be treated with quiet regard, to be granted special shopping privileges or exclusive payment terms, and to be given an easy channel by which to ask questions or deal with other exceptional requests. Just because you know someone's first name and marital status does not mean it's okay to greet him with the equivalent of "Hey, Joe, how's the wife?" Before presuming that your most loyal customers appreciate familiarity, consider how much more they may value their anonymity and privacy.

In fact, most companies realize that displaying too much information about customers before they think the company should have that information can be a real liability, significantly *reducing* response rates. Consider the call center screen pop. Typically, when calling a toll-free customer assistance number, one expects to hear a greeting along the following lines: "Mortgage Headquarters Service Center. How may I direct your call?" Yet given today's technology, the CSR could just as easily answer, "Good morning, Mr. Jones. Would you like to refinance your house in Sludge Falls?" The customer hangs up. What happened? Certain expectations about anonymity and privacy went unfulfilled. Companies need to exercise extreme caution when referring to personal data, unless the customer has explicitly given the company permission to present that information. It's one of the reasons that one-to-one marketing can often be ineffective, and even counterproductive.

The best future loyalty programs will be those that treat their customers like celebrities, in all the best senses of the word. Rather than fawning service and exaggerated familiarity, savvy marketers will create unique, leisurely commercial spaces for their best customers, the equivalent of those after-hours shopping privileges afforded to Hollywood celebrities. What might that look like? Look no further than what retailer J. Crew is already doing. For its best customers, the clothing leader creates special advance sales notices it delivers by e-mail, granting privileged access to online closeouts and seasonal sales.

Future customer loyalty programs will finally achieve cross-channel integration, so that CSRs in any contact center can access data from any channel, and customers can simply do as they please.

Loyal customers may wish to make a purchase on the Web, complete a return in the store, and then order a replacement over the telephone. Many first-generation loyalty programs are investing far too much budget on imprinted tchotchkes and other disposable premiums and far too little budget on achieving cross-channel integration. Those that are addressing integration are too often more concerned with how to initiate cross-channel campaigns and other outbound invade-and-persuade tactics rather than how to optimize the handling of inbound service calls. Precision marketers will open and integrate as many channels as their best customers require, but will only initiate contact through those channels that the customer deems appropriate.

Already, many marketers are devising strategies for leveraging short messaging service (SMS) over their customers' cell phones, even as their back-office and front-office systems operate in a state of disconnected stupor. Precision marketers will undertake the challenging task of integrating their existing channels before devising strategies to exploit emerging channels. Again, this is not a sexy, futuristic scenario. But it is the right one.

Already, Harrah's is seeing the benefits of this level of integration. After stitching together their multi-property data systems they implemented Total Rewards, an integrated loyalty program that rewards clients for their play across all Harrah's properties. Harrah's was then able to open and operate a real-time window for their customers, the eTotal Rewards program. It's the first comprehensive online program in the industry to allow players to check their benefits and comps in real time.

Future customer loyalty programs will not require special cards, key chain attachments, or premium-priced memberships. Instead, these programs and privileges will be automatically extended to a company's best customers within the context of an existing transaction. In much the same way frequent fliers need to do little more to achieve premier status than to fly, customer loyalty program members will need to do little more than continue to patronize their favorite businesses. Loyalty rewards, in one form or another, will simply become an expected feature of every shopping experience.

Not to worry, though. The actual footprint of most loyalty programs will shrink, not expand. With each transaction, the customer will receive an informative, detailed receipt that fulfills the role those bulky airline program mailers are intended to fill. They'll answer the following questions in succinct fashion:

~ How much have I bought and/or participated?
~ How much more do I need to buy or participate to receive a reward of some kind?
~ What value-add am I entitled to *right now*?

The majority of retailers will ditch the vast pouches and elaborate magazines—they're too difficult to cost-justify—and offer customers a more simple interface of immediate value. Grocery stores and other retailers are already offering contextual couponing and personalized receipts. And they're also experimenting with radio-frequency technologies that enable customers and service staff alike to gain live access to more detailed information about the items they're interested in. No sooner do you drop something into your cart or hang it up in the dressing room than the smart reader recognizes and records your action, alerts relevant floor sales personnel, and even brings up additional color choices, sizes, or discount opportunities. Granted, real-time, contextual receipts are a far cry from radio-frequency transmissions during your shopping experience. The point is this: Loyalty programs will no longer be bound—in value or functionality—to a colorful laminated card or a fancy stuffed mailer. Instead, they'll exist as an invisible, consistent, and integrated part of every shopping experience.

And because much of what makes up the future loyalty program will take place within the context of a traditional shopping or transactional experience, the profile of CSRs and salespeople will have to change markedly. Loyal shoppers will deserve and demand to be serviced by educated, skilled, and engaged company representatives. Hourly slackers need not apply. In many industries, this will require a renewed investment in the recruitment and training of dedicated employees who can not only scan a credit card or read a call script, but actually understand the underlying structure and philosophy of the company's loyalty program.

As companies achieve integration and learn to apply a softer hand to their loyalty programs, customer distrust will decrease and participation will increase. One of the most compelling trends we see for future loyalty programs is simply this: Everybody will play ball. When loyalty programs become part of the transaction fabric rather than extracurricular clubs, and when value is consistently created, awarded, and communicated, only the truly privacy-obsessed will dream of opting out.

Much of this increased participation will be a direct result of how companies begin to rethink their loyalty programs. Although most customer loyalty programs were originally invented as rewards programs, the programs of the future can be more accurately described as "value programs." You give us some value, we give you some value. More customer data results in lower prices, time savings, special offers and/or access, and so forth.

SOON, WE'LL ALL BE BELIEVERS

The year is 2004, and tens of millions of people are glued to their TV screens for Superbowl XXXVIII. Following that great American tradition of munching on snacks, drinking beers, and cheering and cursing while rooting for their favorite teams, everyone is deeply immersed in the game's play-by-play action. The skirmishes. The fouls. The passes. The rushes. The touchdowns. By and large, everyone is paying an equal amount of attention to the 30-second commercial spots for which dozens of advertisers, including PepsiCo, Visa, Allstate, FedEx, J.C. Penney, General Motors, Frito-Lay, Anheuser-Busch, Gillette, and Procter & Gamble have each plunked down an average of $2.4 million. For this deep-pocketed group of major marketers, the price tag comes to $80,000 per second of brand-awareness raising. It's what they have to pay, they figure, to keep their brands "top of mind."

Will some things never change? Are companies such creatures of habit that they will continue to engage in mass media marketing in much the same way that they have since 1941, when the first TV commercials began to air, even when the world around them has changed so dramatically over the past six decades—and, particularly, over the past one decade? As we've said, the answer is yes *and* no.

The Superbowl. The World Series. The Academy Awards show. The Grammy Awards show. These programs and a handful of others that draw huge numbers of people—in some cases, more than half the TV viewing audience, across practically every conceivable consumer segment—will continue to sell all of their commercial time months in advance, and for record-breaking sums of money. After all, if in one fell swoop you can reach half the nation's population—a population that is likely to be more attentive than usual (as tends to be the case with these programs, since the commercials boast higher-than-average entertainment value)—then you're guaranteed to reach a large portion of your target audience, no matter their genetic makeup.

Let's do the math. Assume that 100 million people turn on their TVs for Superbowl XXXVIII. Assume, further, that roughly half of them stick around for the commercial breaks. In theory, a major marketer with a prime prospect base composed of 20 percent of the general population would effectively reach five million of those prime prospects at a cost of less than 25 cents per person. In the final analysis, it may be a very affordable price on a cost-per-impression basis, given the alignment of business objectives and the rarity of the opportunity to market to so many target customers en masse.

Meanwhile, of course, 99 percent of the programs on TV fail to attract tens of millions of people, or even a tiny fraction of that number. As the universe of viewers continues to fragment into increasingly smaller pieces, for all the reasons that we've previously stated (cable/satellite channels, DVRs, the Internet), the economics of mass media marketing become *less* attractive and the economics of precision marketing become *more* attractive. This is especially true for products with narrower customer appeal than soft drinks from Pepsi, insurance from Allstate, apparel from J.C. Penney, razor blades from Gillette, and paper towels from P&G. Yet, again, it's not an either/or situation. Knocked from its pedestal as the primary means by which companies can market to consumers, mass media, including not only TV but also radio, magazines, and billboards—as well as a large portion of the $120 billion or so that companies spend on generic direct mail—have, in effect, become *point solutions*. To become part of a *complete solution*, they need to join forces with precision marketing techniques.

Ironically, as we've suggested, the same technologies that diminish TV's potency as a marketing tool are giving birth to a new set of tools that could prove to be far more effective in terms of producing favorable business outcomes. While we've talked about online profiling and contextual advertising on the Web, the true realization of these tools rests on the convergence of the TV and the computer. For a number of years, pundits have prognosticated the imminent convergence of these very different technologies, which are typically used by people for very different purposes. And while it may be a number of years before computers and TVs are able to display the same media in the same format such that people will no longer distinguish between them, the proliferation of broadband connections, the rapid growth of broadband content-delivery services, and the FCC ruling that TVs must go digital by 2006, all suggest that that day may be finally on the horizon.

And what will this convergence mean for precision marketing? It will mean that consumers will be able to invite companies to stream only the most relevant advertisements into their homes, based on their stated interests, their past viewing behavior, and whatever information they choose to make available in their personal profiles. It will mean that, with permission, companies will be able to tap into people's preference engines, based on transaction and interaction data—and perhaps even the transaction databases themselves. Most importantly, perhaps, it will mean that companies will be able to better track the results of their marketing expenditures and better measure their Marketing ROI.

New technologies will unleash a world of possibilities when it comes to enhancing a company's marketing activities, from promotions delivery to campaign management to personalization. Some of the possibilities we can't begin to imagine—how market researchers will use complexity science and agent-based models to build rule-based decision simulations, for example, or how they will use neuromarketing precedures to refine branding effectiveness. But we do know that, despite the infusion of science, the creative aspects of marketing will never go away. Science is only half the battle won. For that matter, marketing itself is only half the battle won. After all, you can bring a horse to water, but at some point that water better taste pretty good.

NOTES

Introduction

1. Interview with Bill Bean by Jeff Zabin, October 21, 2003.
2. "Brand Killers," *Fortune*, August 11, 2003.
3. See "Does the Internet Make Markets More Competitive?" Jeffrey R. Brown, Austan Goolsbee, *NBER Working Paper*, November 2000.
4. Tom Barnes, "Rethinking The Product Life Cycle: Brand And Segment Maturity For The Next Century," *AdvertisingDay*, April 21, 2003. Used by permission.
5. Interview with Dan Collins by Jeff Zabin, June 25, 2003.
6. See the "Survey of Marketing Performance Management," conducted in 2001 by Reveries.com/IntelliSurvey for Veridiem, Inc.

CHAPTER 1 The Rise of Precision Marketing

1. Reporters later documented some of the civilian effects of "precision bombing," noting that injuries and deaths often resulted from misdirected bombs or from fragments that sprayed into homes even when the munitions found their intended target. Such reports offer a sobering view of "precision" in a war context.
2. These jokes are attributed to Henny Youngman, Rodney Dangerfield, and George Burns, respectively.
3. See Wendell Smith, "Product Differentiation and Market Segmentation as Alternative Marketing Strategies," *Journal of Marketing*. July 1956.

4. See Theodore Levitt, *Marketing for Business Growth* (McGraw-Hill, 1974).

5. Interview with Marc Landsberg by Jeff Zabin, June 15, 2003.

6. Michael Lewis, "Boom Box," *New York Times Magazine*, August 13, 2000. The content subsequently appeared in the book *Next: The Future Just Happened* (W.W. Norton & Company, 2001). This excerpt is reprinted with permission from Michael Lewis.

7. Ibid.

8. Nick Cavnar, Vice President, Circulation, Intertec Publishing, as quoted in the article "Folio: Plus," *Folio:* magazine, January 1, 2001.

9. Interview with Mike Dobbs by Jeff Zabin, July 14, 2003.

10. Mohan Sawhney originally coined the term "the myth of substitution" in his essay "Hand In Hand" in *Context Magazine*, April/May 2000. The idea was subsequently expanded by Mohan Sawhney and Jeff Zabin in *The Seven Steps to Nirvana: Strategic Insights Into eBusiness Transformation* (McGraw-Hill, 2001).

11. From "The Future of Simulated Test Markets," by Joseph Willke, President, ACNielsen BASES, published on the ACNielsen website, 2002.

12. Interview with Mike Dobbs by Jeff Zabin, July 14, 2003.

CHAPTER 2   The Precision Marketing Cycle

1. Interview with Mike Duffy by Jeff Zabin, June 27, 2003.

2. Ibid.

3. Interview with Sunil Garga by Jeff Zabin, July 8, 2003.

4. Interview with Bill Bean by Jeff Zabin, October 21, 2003.

5. Interview with Marc Landsberg by Jeff Zabin, June 15, 2003.

6. Interview with Scott Moore by Jeff Zabin, June 25, 2003.

7. See PRIMEDIA's *2003 Promotional Trends* report.

8. Interview with Bill Mirbach by Jeff Zabin, July 7, 2003.

9. Ibid.

10. Interview with Bill Bean by Jeff Zabin, October 21, 2003.

11. Comcast was a 19th Annual Gold Mark Award Winner for its "Segmented 2001 Campaign." See the Cable & Telecommunications Association for Marketing website for further information about past award winners.

12. Interview with Randy Quinn by Jeff Zabin, July 10, 2003.
13. Interview with Mike Dobbs by Jeff Zabin, July 14, 2003.
14. Interview with Mike Duffy by Jeff Zabin, June 27, 2003.
15. Ibid.
16. Interview with David Ormesher by Jeff Zabin, October 24, 2003.
17. For an in-depth discussion of relationship life cycles, see Mohan Sawhney and Jeff Zabin, "Managing and Measuring Relational Equity in the Network Economy," *Journal of the Academy of Marketing Science*, Fall 2002.
18. Dale Carnegie, *How to Win Friends and Influence People* (Pocket Books, 1990).
19. For a more complete discussion of the profit potential initiative at Bridgestone/Firestone, see "Bridgestone/Firestone Minds the Gap," *Direct* magazine, September 1, 2002.
20. Printed with permission from Jonah Peretti.
21. Interview with Peter Zollo by Jeff Zabin, October 24, 2003.

CHAPTER 3   Exploiting the Data

1. Interview with Mike Duffy by Jeff Zabin, June 27, 2003.
2. Interview with Bill Mirbach by Jeff Zabin, July 7, 2003.
3. A final element of functionality in the CFAS is the content manager, which we purposely omit for the sake of simplifying the discussion. The content manager ensures that all of the customer communications materials—from product catalogs to marketing collateral—remain centralized, current, consistent, and easily accessible to the appropriate end users.

CHAPTER 4   Precision Marketing in the Age of Gaia

1. James Lovelock, *Gaia: A New Look at Life on Earth* (Oxford University Press, 1979).
2. The *extended business network* is the system of relationships that a company creates to source, deliver, and augment its offerings. There are several variations on the theme. For example, James Moore, in *Death*

of Competition (John Wiley & Sons, 1996), refers to the structure as *ecosystems*; Don Tapscott et al. in *Digital Capital* (Harvard Business School Press, 2000), uses the term *business webs*; and Gary Hamel in *Leading the Revolution* (Harvard Business School Press, 2001), uses the term *value networks*.

CHAPTER 5   Fifteen Minutes of Privacy?

1. Hearing before the Subcommittee on Commerce, Trade, and Consumer Protection of the Committee on Energy and Commerce, House of Representatives, 107th Cong., 1st sess., July 26, 2001, no. 107–149.
2. Interview with Bill Mirdach by Jeff Zabin, July 7, 2003.
3. Hearing before the Subcommittee on Commerce, Trade, and Consumer Protection of the Committee on Energy and Commerce, House of Representatives, 107th Cong., 1st sess., July 26, 2001, no. 107–149.
4. W.J. "Billy" Tauzin, Chairman, the Committee on Energy and Commerce, Hearing before the Subcommittee on Commerce, Trade, and Consumer Protection, September 24, 2002, on *H.R. 4678, The Consumer Privacy Protection Act of 2002.*
5. Hearing before the Subcommittee on Commerce, Trade, and Consumer Protection of the Committee on Energy and Commerce, House of Representatives, 107th Cong., 1st sess., July 26, 2001, no. 107–149.
6. Kevin Kelly, *Out of Control: The New Biology of Machines, Social Systems and the Economic World* (Perseus Publishing, 1995).
7. Hearing before the Subcommittee on Commerce, Trade, and Consumer Protection of the Committee on Energy and Commerce, House of Representatives, 107th Cong., 1st sess., July 26, 2001, no. 107–149.

CHAPTER 6   The Precision Marketing Future

1. As quoted in the article "The Future According to Spielberg: *Minority Report* and the World of Ubiquitous Computing," *M-Pulse*

magazine, published by the Hewlett-Packard Company, August 2002.

2. Interview with Jeff Boortz by Jeff Zabin, July 21, 2003.
3. Ibid.
4. "Bigger Monster, Weaker Chains: The Growth of an American Surveillance Society," a report published by the American Civil Liberties Union, January 13, 2003.

INDEX

ABOUT THE AUTHORS

Jeff Zabin is Director of Marketing in the Global Marketing Solutions group at Fair Isaac Corporation, the leading provider of customer analytics and decision technology. A widely recognized business thinker, he is the coauthor of *The Seven Steps to Nirvana: Strategic Insights into eBusiness Transformation* (McGraw-Hill, 2001). He has written for several trade magazines, and his research has been published in leading practitioner and academic journals, including the *Journal of the Academy of Marketing Science.* He is also a frequent keynote speaker for business forums in the United States and Europe. A graduate of the University of Wisconsin, and a returned Peace Corps volunteer, Jeff lives with his wife and two children in Evanston, Illinois, and is often included in lists of Chicago's most influential IT professionals.

Gresh Brebach is Managing Director of The Brebach Group, a consultancy specializing in marketing services and enterprise performance management. A recognized authority on transforming businesses by aligning corporate strategies with organizational structures, operating processes, and IT infrastructures, he has both managed large-scale businesses and founded three start-ups, two resulting in successful IPOs. As a former Director in the New York office of McKinsey & Co., he led the firm's North American IT practice. Gresh also served as the Managing

Partner of the North American consulting practice of Andersen Consulting (Accenture). He earned his BS in Engineering and MBA from the University of Illinois, and also currently serves on the board of directors for Aspen Technology, Inc. He lives with his wife in Marblehead, Massachusetts.

For more information about Fair Isaac, visit www.fairisaac.com.